The Sunday After

By Reverend Gary B. Agee

Spirit Wind Books
P.O. Box 148
West Elkton, Ohio 45070

The Sunday After
Living With Tragedy
This Side Of America's Worst Day

Reverend Gary B. Agee

Acknowledgements

Many thanks to my patient wife who shouldered most of the responsibility of our young family as I went chasing yet another dream. And to my children who bear with their "poppa," I bless you in the name of Jesus. To those with whom I spend my Sundays, thank you for loving me as I am.

The most horrible tragedy ever to occur in the Christian psyche occurred on the day that its' Founder, its' favorite Son, its' King was murdered. God in His wondrous kindness and good will toward the people He had created sent, a Savior to be with them, to lead them, to teach and to redeem them. Ultimate good, met the free choice of humanity at that pivotal moment two thousand years ago. People no better nor worse than you and I chose to do violence to an innocent man, Jesus the Divine One was crucified on Friday. This disaster brought the fledgling church to the edge of despair. Had it not been for God who intervened in such a marvelous and wonderful way, the church could not have survived. The violence and evil of a fallen world was radically superseded by the resurrection of Jesus Christ. The resurrection took place on "the Sunday after."

Preface

Following the horrific events of September 11, 2001, I felt a book should be produced that would examine how the pastors and leaders of the Church of God Reformation Movement handled the September 11th terrorist strikes in pulpits across the United States of America. No matter how one measures the terrorist strikes of September 11, 2001, whether it be by the number of civilians murdered, by the value of property destroyed or by the sheer terror experienced by the citizens of the world's last remaining superpower, these attacks were the most violent and devastating attacks ever perpetrated against the citizens of this nation. My original idea was to review about fifty audio and videotapes of worship services held in Church of God congregations from around the country in order to find out what the movement thought about the crises and how they in turn responded through their preaching and prayers especially in the September 16th services, the Sunday immediately following the September 11th terrorist strikes. I originally planned to produce a more academic work with the intent of exploring how effectively the Church of God Reformation Movement addressed this national tragedy. Did we as a movement do all right? I think this original plan, though later adjusted, was a good one. The Church of God Reformation Movement, which some have described as a "heart" movement, would certainly do well to spend some time and energy "thinking" and reflecting on this unprecedented national tragedy and our response to this tragedy. We must, in short, periodically examine how effectively we are addressing a world full of hurting individuals living through frightening and chaotic times in desperate need of the gospel of Hope. The events of September 11th seem to call for this type of reflective evaluation. I trust someone will take up the academic task of critically examining how effectively the Church of God Reformation Movement responded to the terrorist strikes of September 11, 2001. Should someone decide to step forward to answer this challenge, I would raise the following questions related to the terrorist strikes and the Church of God's subsequent response for consideration:

1. Was what we sung, prayed and preached relevant for the people seeking help in a time of unprecedented national tragedy?
2. Did we as a movement see these events through the lens of God's Word? Did we see them as God saw them?
3. Are we prepared as a movement to address the questions and concerns faced by the people in our communities both inside and outside of the church? Do we know what these questions are?
4. Could we as a movement be better prepared to deal with similar terrorist strikes against this nation, which are certain to follow?
5. Do the pastors and leaders of the Church of God Reformation need further dialogue with people of other cultures and faiths? How might this be done with integrity given our evangelical convictions?
6. What does it mean to confess that God loves the world? Do we as a movement love the world outside the walls of the church, outside the borders of this country? How might the carrying out of the Great Commission change our hearts as believers in Christ?
7. Are we as a movement capable of winning the world for Christ? Is there a place for listening and learning in our evangelical mission programs?
8. In what areas do we need to repent and grow as a movement? Are we willing to make the necessary changes God may be asking us to make in a changing and uncertain world?

After some soul searching and many hours of research, writing and reflecting, I have decided not to do a critical academic study of the Reformation Movement's response to the September 11, 2001, terrorist strikes. Instead, I thought it would be more fruitful to bring to light the helpful insights and lessons drawn from this national tragedy; specifically, those insights and lessons that might help people through times when they are experiencing personal tragedy. The collective wisdom and insight initially shared with respective congregations in the form of messages, sermons and prayers in the days immediately following the September 11th attacks contains a healing agent. I am confident after many hours reviewing these messages and prayers, that the insights and lessons shared by pastors and church leaders across the Church of God Reformation Movement following this horrific tragedy will be helpful for individuals facing personal tragedy; be that a serious illness, the loss of a loved one, the pain of a broken relationship, etc. It is my desire that this book will meet the following three objects:

The first, is to give an account of what useful lessons and perspectives regarding tragedy one might draw from the fifty or so worship services surveyed in this study. What did we as individuals, pastors, leaders and lay people alike learn from this national tragedy that could be applied in a way that would bring help and healing to the people that experience, far too frequently, personal tragedies in our congregations?

The second objective is to leave for posterity a written record of some of the prayers lifted and the messages delivered in churches across the U.S. during those dark days of terror and mourning immediately following the terrorist strikes of September 11th.

Perhaps some inquiring PhD a hundred years hence will want to begin an exploration of the impact of the September 11th terrorist strikes on the life of the Church of God Reformation Movement. I would be thrilled to think that this book might provide a starting point.

The third, and final, objective for this book will be more difficult to meet - though no less inspirational. During this research, I have immensely enjoyed reviewing worship tapes from churches all over the continental United States, from urban centers like Brooklyn, New York; Atlanta, Georgia; Phoenix, Arizona; and Chicago, Illinois, to smaller cities like Meridian, Mississippi; Middletown, Ohio; and Anchorage, Alaska. In addition, I have received material from rural communities like Peebles, Ohio: and Hatch, New Mexico. I have found a joy in the discovery of just how diverse we are as a movement. Some churches had very free worship services with a contemporary worship style. Others churches featured a more formal worship atmosphere with a thundering pipe organ supporting the rich, traditional hymns of this movement's history. The Spirit of God, and the life He brings, seemed to be active in all of the tapes I reviewed. Blessed are we in our diversity. I trust a bit of the beauty of that diversity will show through the pages of this manuscript, a diversity that we would do well to celebrate.

I am very aware of the limitations of this book. First of all, it is very difficult to reduce a three dimensional work like a sermon with all of its non-verbal nuances, down to a written text without leaving behind much that is valuable. I trust not too much is lost in this transfer. I am confident that some of the passion and feeling, which at times led me to tears as I listened, will come through in the written prayers and messages cited in this book.[1] A second limitation is the fact that I did not, in a major way, address the musical selections chosen and performed on the Sundays immediately following the September 11th terrorist strikes. We are a singing people. What was sung certainly gives insight into what convictions we held as a movement at this critical time in the life of our nation. Although a study of the music would have been insightful and helpful in how the movement processed this national tragedy, this type of study was beyond my time parameters. A third limitation of this book is the lack of entries from outside the United States and Canada. The fact is, I found it difficult to make the contacts necessary to include offerings in this book from pastors and churches outside of North America. I am quite sure that had I been able to establish contacts with Church of God leaders overseas, this book would have been even richer and more diverse. A fourth limitation of this book is that it was rushed to press. I felt it was important to get the book into the public's hands as close to the first year anniversary of the terrorist strikes of September 11 as was humanly possible. Deadlines kept the project moving forward at a pace with which I was not always comfortable. I am inclined to believe that producing a good manuscript is similar to preparing a tasty pasta sauce – they both need plenty of time to simmer. In the months I

---

[1] Some of the sermons and talks delivered on September 11th were incredibly moving. Art Kelly, Church of God Ministries, suggested during my time of research that it might be a good idea to make this collection of September 11th sermons available on CD. Though outside of my field of expertise, I heartily endorse the idea.

took to research and write this book, what I found was no surprise. As a full-time pastor, and parent of six children (two in diapers), there are precious few minutes in each day available for deep reflection and writing. I trust these limitations have not seriously hurt this book and I invite others who are more qualified and have more available time to add to this study.

Night Is Broken

All is night, dark and still, nature groans in expectation.
A solitary beaked melody breaks night's hold, a prophet's song of
hope.
A solo first, then a chorus of varied winged fowl sing in
anticipation.
The song of approaching day, too sweet to be quieted longer –
Bursts Forth.

Darkness flees from east to west as the light from Earth's closest
star
Sets sky and nearby clouds aflame – Victorious Assent.

Night, the bridled beast, again forced into exile by
our Maker
Before watering eyes and trembling hearts.

Then release your hold vanquished night;
Sing on winged prophets of Hope
From your watchman's perch with eyes fixed on the sky.

Night is broken, day approaches.

- Gary Agee

Table of Contents

When Words Are Hard To Come By:
An Introduction

June 1, 1991.

I have kept a journal for several years. I always enjoy first recording, and then when I feel so inclined, rereading entries detailing events momentous and mundane alike, recalling the names and faces of interesting people and beautiful places during my life's journey. However, immediately after May 17, 1991, the entries into my journal for some time were greatly curtailed. For on that day, at 1:40 PM, my wife, Lori, and I welcomed into the world, a few weeks premature, our firstborn son, Jacob Ryan Agee. Because of my wife's medical condition at that time, he came by emergency Cesarean Section. In my journal, I record the events of that day. "The baby's health looks good according to the pediatrician...etc."

A few days later, the baby began to experience some difficulties with his circulatory system. The doctors must have known instinctively that it was very serious because Jake was sent immediately to a pediatric care facility in a neighboring city. Hours later, my wife, a new mother, and I, a rookie father, heard the words that no parent ever wants to hear. "I am sorry. I have some terrible news, your baby is going to die." God, that still has an awful ring to it!

Lori and I were permitted to bring Jake home. Amazingly, he lived two weeks. We cared for our little boy though as we carried him, we tried to push into the recesses of our mind the fact that in a matter of hours he would be dead. My journal does not record the events of Jacob's short life, or the details of the fourteen days that Lori and I shared with him. Maybe some of the events of these days were simply too dark to encode at the time. For example, the night Lori had been feeding Jacob, when he started choking on the formula. My exhausted wife stood over me, tears streaming down her face, crying, "I killed my baby." Or, when the funeral director placed our son in what looked to be a lunch box as he prepared to carry him to the car to be put in his trunk. In his trunk, like a sack of groceries. For a new mother, that was just too much to bear. Lori had to be escorted out of

I

the room. I remember the day when we buried Jake; I carried that tiny casket to the graveside. No words could adequately describe the loss of Jacob. In my journal, the silence was broken on June 1, the day we buried my son. I could muster only these words written in green marker beneath two dried cotton swabs taped to the page, swabs that had been used to moisten Jake's mouth on his last day with us:

June 1, 1991
Today my son died. What more need be said.

Half a man that's all I am—
Just half and nothing more,
For the half of me that careless went—
Lives with me no more.

September 16, A Day When Words Did Not Come Easy

Lesson 1: When Tragedy Strikes,
Words Are Hard To Come By

One of the interesting things I discovered from reviewing the tapes of services around the country, was the honesty and vulnerability heard in the voices of pastors. These leaders who are charged with declaring the Word of God, brought light and hope to their respective congregations in the days immediately following the tragic events of September 11, 2001. It was evident that many of the pastors and church leaders themselves were having a difficult time processing this national tragedy. As I did the research for this book, it was apparent that the members of the clergy felt the same shock, fear, disorientation, and confusion that their parishioners were experiencing. Most also recognized that a mere sermon, a collection of words, even words of faith and hope about God, seemed so inadequate to address the deep pain and hurt people all across the nation were feeling following the terrorist strikes of September 11, 2001. Consider some of the following comments:

Bob Marvel from Bellingham, Washington, shared these words as he began his message the Sunday after the terrorist strikes of September 11th:
"This week, we have experienced the worst tragedy in the history of our country. No doubt, individually and collectively, we have been sent reeling by the impact. We have been gripped with disbelief and shock. We have been gripped with sorrow and anger; we have been gripped with fear and with questions. It has been a very difficult and heavy week."[2]

Ken Long related the following story about how a pastor in California reacted after receiving the news that President John F. Kennedy had been shot:

---

[2] Bob Marvel. "Living on a Prayer." Bellingham, Washington. September 16, 2001.

"He climbed to the top of his tower at his church and began to just ring the bell. And he just pulled that rope and rang the bell as long as he could until he was exhausted. He said when he climbed down and went into his sanctuary, it was full of people who had tears in their eyes and they were just sitting there looking at him wondering what is he going to say. I thought about that this week. What are we going to say? I know that times like this are very unique…The temptation in a pastor is to try to answer some of these questions. As you well know, we can't really do that. There aren't a lot of answers. When Billy Graham, after eighty faithful years of service, can stand before a congregation, before a whole nation and say I don't know the answer…Then I'm not going to presume to know that answer."[3]

Paul Mumaw shared the following with his congregation after the deadly terrorist strikes of September 11th:

"I am sure that there are many of you here that would remember the Pearl Harbor bombings sixty years ago. And you can probably remember where you were the day you received the news. And the Kennedy assassination in the sixties…so many people seem to remember that exact moment. I can remember the Space Shuttle Challenger exploding over the skies of Florida as a young student and watching it on television. Or, the moment [President George H. Bush] committed troops to the Persian Gulf War and the impact that it had on my life. I'll remember sitting at Lincoln Land Community College in a health class when we received the news that the Oklahoma City bombing had taken place. I'll remember my lunch break a few years ago when I came home from Anderson University and I sat and watched the news of the disaster unfolding at Columbine High School. But in all my life, I will never forget where I was on Tuesday, September 11, 2001, when I received the news that the World Trade Center Towers were coming down and the Pentagon had been badly damaged. And that another plane had fallen from the sky in Pennsylvania. Where were you on Tuesday? I think September 11th

---

[3] Ken Long. "How to Handle Difficult Times." Vero Beach, Florida. September 16, 2001.

will be a day that you will remember for as long as you live…. I was down at Bethel College with Pastor Jim taking a graduate class on Tuesday, Wednesday and Thursday. I knew my wife would be home over lunch break. And I really wanted to talk to her, to see if she was doing all right. She was. I wanted to be able to hear her voice and to encourage one another… I am sure you looked for those same words of comfort as well. It has been a difficult week."[4]

Mitchell Burch felt the need to step away from his pulpit in order to communicate the love of God in a more personal way the Sunday following the assaults on the World Trade Center and the Pentagon:

"I wish we were sitting around your coffee table talking. But because I can't go to every one of you and embrace you and talk personally to everyone of you, I thought I would get the pulpit out of the way. I don't feel too preachy this morning. I love to preach and that's my heart, but I don't feel that this morning. I feel like an inadequate pastor. That's what I feel. And so, with that perspective, I just want to share with you a few thoughts this morning, a few things I feel like God has said to me in the last few days. When I have asked him, as probably all of you have asked him. 'Why God? Why did this happen? How did it happen? What's going to happen?' All of those questions swirl so viciously around my mind. Each of us has been struggling with heart issues that have surfaced during this tragic week in our nation's life. As we pondered the pain, and the anger, and the frustration, the fear in our hearts, I for one, have tried to ask God to teach me something…I have not suffered in comparison to the suffering and the anguish that's going on in D.C and in New York and in other parts of the world…In a lot of ways, I feel unqualified to talk about it. In fact, I don't remember in the twenty-five years of my ministry, preaching specifically from this subject in this way." [5]

---

[4] Paul Mumaw. "The Open Arms of Jesus." St. Joseph, Michigan. September 16, 2001

[5] Mitchell Burch. "The Problem of Suffering." Vancouver, Washington. September 16, 2001.

Jeff Mugford, from the Mountain Park Community Church in Phoenix, Arizona, expressed the following comments in the early worship service as the congregation anxiously awaited the return from New York City of Senior Pastor Robin Wood. Who, when the attacks of September 11th occurred, was staying only blocks from the World Trade Center.

"A former student, now at the University of Arizona, sent me an E-mail several hours after the tragedy this week. I want to share just a couple of excerpts from it, because I think he certainly described what I was feeling and maybe what you have felt too."

"I have deep questions Pastor Jeff. I have no answers. Why us? Why now? What have we done as a nation to endure such an act of violence? I know and understand that you have no answers, and are as shocked as I am. What about the rightfulness and Godly aspects of this issue? For the first time in my life, I am doubting God. I cannot fathom a God who would allow such deeds. I am lost in confusion and hate. I watch the news and I feel nothing but hate toward all parties responsible whoever they may be. Is this right? I can't help it. I feel that I have tried to look at every aspect presented. I still cannot come up with a plausible cause for this magnitude of destruction. I find myself seeking revenge against countries or even sole persons. I wish them death. And at the same token I feel ashamed, because I know that was not the way I was raised by my parents, and what I have learned from the Bible and from you, Jeff, at 'Hot Church.' As you can see, I am in a state of disarray. Any advice, Scripture or words of encouragement would sure be helpful."[6]

Dan Pinter discussed with obvious emotional overload the effect the September 11th terrorist strikes had on him personally, even as he attempted to reach out and provide comfort and hope to the members of his flock:

"Personally I have been struggling with what do I say this morning? What can I give? First of all, how can I give? Because, I feel like I

---

[6] Jeff Mugford. "Questions You Will Answer." Phoenix, Arizona. September 16, 2001.

have been drained dry. What can I say at a time like this? I can't say anything. Today, I am going to do something I know that I have never done before. All I want to do this morning is to read Scripture. If you want to follow along, I will tell you where we are going... Let the Word of God minister to you. I don't know how long this will take; it may take thirty minutes; it may take ten. I don't know. The images that are burned into my mind are the images of those two towers as they both individually began to collapse and fall. That is a picture I know I will never forget. But I am reminded of a passage of Scripture that reminds us that 'the name of the Lord is a strong tower, the righteous run to it and they are saved'."[7]

Many Church of God pastors across the country struggled with whether to go forward with a preaching series scheduled prior to the September 11th terrorist strikes. A large number of pastors chose, after some reflection and prayer, to stick with what they had originally planned. Consider a few of the following examples:

Rod Stafford, from the Fairfax Community Church in Fairfax, Virginia, shared this rationale for his decision:
"One of the other questions that I have gotten a lot this week is, 'Rod, are we going to do anything special in this weekend worship service when we come together?' My response to that has been the same. My response is, we do not have to do anything special. The worship service that we have planned, and had planned for weeks, speaks directly to what we are going through and the tragedy that has taken place and our response to that as a people of God. Let me just remind you of what already was planned weeks before ... We are in the midst of a five week series. The focus of that series is discovering the essential equipment for life. What is essential for life? When you look at the grand scheme of things and you kind of boil everything down to what is really important, what really is important for us? We talked last week about one of the essentials for life: passionately worshipping the invincible, unassailable God of the universe. One of

---

[7] Dan Pinter. "Is God Big Enough…To Bless Me?" September 16, 2001.

the essentials of life is building upon the unshakable foundation of God's word. Next week, we will be talking about building true community, having relationships in which the character and the quality really matter, relationships that go beneath just the surface level of friendship. The following week, we will be talking about discovering your purpose in life and using your life to fulfill the purpose for which God created you. Fifthly, one of the essentials is letting God use our lives to tell other persons about the life saving gospel of Jesus Christ. In light of what has happened this past week, some of you may be here today, and you are reevaluating those things. And you are saying, 'Yeah, what really is essential in my life?' What really is important in my life? When you strip everything away, what really are the important things of life?" [8]

Dr. G. David Cox, from Indiana shared:
"Well, I have struggled a bit this week. I have considered the thought of completely changing the direction of my sermon for today. But, I have thought again and I am going to continue with my series from the life of Joseph, partly because I believe that it would be God's plan for us just to go right on."

Some ministers, on the other hand, felt that the Lord was leading them to set aside scheduled topics in order that they might address directly the events of September 11th.

Paul Sheppard expressed his thoughts to his congregation regarding setting aside his scheduled sermon series in order to give a Biblical perspective to the events of September 11th:
"I am in the midst of a sermon series in the early part of the book of the Revelation. But, in the wake of this past week's events, I feel absolutely compelled to suspend that series today and to speak directly to the church and to those who would listen to this message on tape or

---

[8] Rod Stafford. "Discovering God's Purpose for Your Life." September 16, 2001.

by means of radio. I trust this message will be a timely word as we seek to gain some sense of perspective in light of these events."[9]

Greg Smith shared this conviction with his congregation upon his return to his flock September 23, 2001:

"At three o'clock last Thursday afternoon I felt pretty strongly that the Lord was telling me to change the message that I had planned for the week. Now, for me who is the kind of guy who has everything outlined months ahead, that is a little unnerving. You know we are in the midst of a Matthew message series, and there was a word planned for this day. But, I sensed very strongly a different word particularly in light of what has taken place in our world today. So, if you will just bear with me, we will get back to Matthew next week if you don't mind." [10]

Though these words may have been hard to come by, and though at times the pastors in our pulpits weren't exactly certain just what word they were to share following the terrorist strikes, the focus of the remainder of this book is to get at the truth communicated by these same pastors from the Church of God Reformation Movement. In most cases, these truths were spoken on the Sunday after America's worst day, September 11, 2001. What did we have to say when people flocked back to church in record numbers on "the Sunday After?" It is my conviction that much of what was said in the pulpits around the country could help sustain individuals as they face the personal tragedies that visit every life from time to time. My hope is that the

---

[9] Paul Sheppard. "An American Tragedy In Biblical Perspective." Menlo Park, California. September 16, 2001.

[10] Greg Smith. Birmingham, Alabama. September 23, 2001. Greg spent some time counseling families of victims and rescue workers at Ground Zero following the terrorist strikes of September 11th.

lessons and insights spread across the seven chapters of this book may indeed be of some help as you persevere through tragedy.

Chapter One
I Come To The Garden

"One of the things I have appreciated about our President has been his level-headedness and the fact that he has looked to the Lord for direction, and he has called us as a body of people to do that.... One thing is for sure; the [American] Civil Liberties Union has been very quiet; they are letting us pray everywhere, in the courthouses, on the lawn, in schools, anywhere you want to pray... I am so glad about it."

Dr. Rita Johnson
Sumpter Community Church of God
Belleville, Michigan

"I am concerned this week because we have, as our President said this week, been stirred to anger by this violent act. I feel moved to pray for our leaders. We should have been doing it all along. We should have been disciplined in praying for our leaders. But right now they need our prayers. There are decisions being made that are so important and critical. There are people's lives at stake. When the bombs start falling, and the troops start moving in, people's lives will be disrupted in a major way. Let us pray for our leaders."

Gary Agee
Hopewell First Church of God
West Chester, Ohio

Lesson 2: When Tragedy Strikes, Pray!

One of the primary lessons we learned following the September 11, 2001, terrorist strikes on the United States, was how much prayer means to us as people when we find ourselves facing tragedy. Whether one is a believer or an unbeliever it really makes little difference. People are wired to call out to God in trouble. It is almost a knee jerk reaction. In some ways, I think telling people to pray, when they feel their world is coming a part is like telling a starving person to eat. I

1

have a friend who does not attend church. He rarely calls, but when he finds himself facing a crisis, he calls and asks for prayer.

In a hastily arranged prayer service, held the evening of September 11th, the Reverend Mitchell Burch from Vancouver, Washington, shared with his congregation his own story of how he felt the need and then went to prayer as he witnessed the calamitous events of September 11th unfolding:

"This morning, at about fifteen until six, I was going about my day like everyone else...doing what I typically do in the routine of my life. I was at Remo's Club, and I looked up at the TV screen. The World Trade Center in New York City, New York, was on fire. Initially, I couldn't hear the report; I just heard that there had been an explosion. I immediately prayed God be with those who were there and those working. Moments later, the news said it was actually a terrorist attack with the airplane, and then about sixteen or seventeen minutes later I saw with my own eyes live on television the second airplane." [11]

In Reverend Burch's Sunday morning service, he shared the following account, which illuminates an almost immediate impulse to go to prayer. This impulse was felt not only by the pastor, but also by other members of the club as they watched, live, the tragic events of September 11th unfold:

"I had just stepped on a treadmill at the club to work out that morning. It was about quarter until six. I turned around and saw CNN on TV. I saw smoke coming out of one of the towers. I thought, 'There's a fire at the Trade Center.' Shortly after that, news reporters were talking about a plane that flew into it. Immediately, we were thrust into this catastrophic moment. Then a few moments later, as I was watching the report, I saw live on television the second aircraft come through and hit the second tower. I had people on the [equipment] behind me, the stair masters in front of me, and on the treadmills beside me, and they all stopped. I got off my treadmill and I

---

[11] Mitchell Burch. September 11th Prayer Service. Vancouver, Washington. September 11, 2001.

2

hit my knees beside the treadmill. I wasn't praying loud or even out loud. I was just saying, 'Dear God, whatever's happening, help us.' A couple of people were around me too. I didn't hear what they were praying, but they were in a posture of prayer."[12]

John Spear discussed with his congregation this same willingness and desire felt on the part of people to turn to God for help in prayer following the terrorist strikes of September 11th:

"One of the good things that has been remarkable is the way in which people are seeking refuge in God. Prayer groups are going on all around the world, in every community, and in every city. It was a very encouraging thing for me as a pastor to be a part of a prayer group here at a city park at noon on Friday, and to see the hundreds of people who came to the biggest community gathering of its kind that I have seen in the eleven years that I have been here. People who came together, and prayed together, were seeking refuge in God. Our television is full of it. Individuals are expressing their hearts… and interceding for others. They are asking God for His help in a very discouraging time. On Friday, the political leaders of both parties of both houses of Congress, military leaders, individuals, and influential people met together in the National Cathedral in Washington, D.C., for a service, and were addressed by the Rev. Billy Graham, our President, and representatives of the Catholic, Jewish, and Muslim faiths. It was very obvious that people were seeking refuge in God in the midst of this national tragedy."[13]

Jonah

As has been illustrated above, when people get into trouble, they pray. It is the type of response we see in so many Biblical passages. Consider the story of Jonah. Jonah had been called by God to go and minister to the great city of Nineveh, the capital of the Assyrian Empire. Because he had no compassion for these people, he flatly

---

[12] Mitchell Burch. Vancouver, Washington. September 16, 2001.
[13] John Spear. "Journey to the Heart of God." Casper, Wyoming. September 16, 2001.

refused. Instead, he boarded a boat bound for Tarshish to run from the presence of the Lord. Tragedy then visited the life of Jonah and his unsuspecting traveling companions. In Jonah 1:4-5, we read:

"And the Lord hurled a great wind on the sea and there was a great storm on the sea so that the ship was about to break up. Then the sailors became afraid and every man cried to his god."

Jonah is chided in verse seven for sleeping during the storm, and was urged, "Get up, call on your God."

After every attempt to row the ship to safety, Jonah 1:13-15 reads, "The sea was becoming even stormier against them. Then they called on the Lord and said, 'We earnestly pray, O Lord, do not let us perish on account of this man's life and do not put innocent blood on us: for Thou, O Lord, hast done as Thou hast pleased.' So they picked up Jonah and threw him into the sea, and the sea stopped its raging."

At that point, it is easy to imagine that Jonah was experiencing despair. His future was bleak. He would be tossed overboard and, no doubt, down into the dark raging sea, almost certainly he would drown. The desperate place in which Jonah found himself was tragic. Seeing no way out, he did what, I believe, is instinctive for all of God's children - those inside and outside the church. He called out to the Lord. Jonah 2:1 reads:

"Then Jonah prayed to the Lord his God from the stomach of the fish… God heard Jonah's prayer." [14]

---

[14] Following the Tragedy of September 11th, I spent some time doing a study of the book of Jonah. There are many insights that I gained from this effort carried out in the shadow of 9/11. Scholars tell us that the book of Jonah was intended to be a direct frontal assault against those people in the Jewish religion who held to the conviction that God's favor rested exclusively on the Jews. Sadly, many evangelical Christians unwittingly have adopted this same favored status vis a vi the world. The book of Jonah forces us to take seriously a God who cares for those outside of the "evangelical flock." He really does, in fact, love the world. As one works through the pages of this powerful book, it is Jonah, God's prophet, who is the one out of line and consequently in need of adjustment. The book is really about God attempting to convert Jonah to a heart of compassion for the world. This effort takes up the major part of the book; a real irony when one considers that the book recounts the

Jesus

In the closing chapters of all four gospels of the New Testament, Jesus faced a climate that grew worse by the moment. In Luke's account of the crucifixion, we see Jesus as the dark storm clouds

---

remarkable conversion of the whole population of the city of Nineveh in only a few verses. In each chapter God seems to highlight the virtues of the "non-believer" over the rebelliousness of his own prophet, Jonah. In chapter one, it is the foreign sailors who call the sleeping Jonah to prayer. In chapter one Jonah runs from his mission to rescue the people of Nineveh because he has no compassion for them; yet in this same chapter the pagan sailors who do not know Jonah, and whose lives were put at risk because of the prophet's disobedience, show him incredible mercy. In chapter one the sailors do all in their power to save Jonah's life. In chapter three the people of the city of Nineveh repent immediately after when they hear the message of Jonah one time. This willingness on the part of the people of Nineveh to repent stands in stark contrast to the waywardness of Israel and the people of God's unwillingness to repent from their own wicked ways despite the repeated warnings of Israel's many prophets. Finally, in chapter four, we find that God draws a parallel between the vine that brought Jonah so much joy, and the city of Nineveh, a pagan city that we are led to believe brought God incredible pleasure. The question remains how might these truths affect our relationship with the unbelieving world. The fact is, that Jonah had the truth but he did not have a heart of compassion for those he was called to win. It seems obvious that God wanted to change the hearts of the disciples when He gave them the Great Commission. As the disciples moved out from Jerusalem, into Judea, through Samaria and into the far reaches of the world, God knew that they would encounter people of increasingly different faiths and cultures. His desire was that those disciples as believers in Christ would fall in love with the people that they were called to win to the faith. God's desire is the same for the disciple today. God's intention is that we would love the world He already loves deeply, profoundly and in a way that we will never completely understand. God is at work yet on converting the believer to his own heart. Merely beaming a satellite signal to the world doesn't accomplish what God intended to do in the life of the believer, or in the world. The story of God's attempt to change the heart of Jonah is similar to the Father's attempt to win over the heart of the elder brother in the prodigal story recorded in Luke chapter fifteen. In both cases we aren't sure if a heart of compassion promoted by God in the book of Jonah, or by the Father in the Lucan account ever born into the lives of these two would be converts. It remains an open question as well for the Church of God Movement as it does for the Evangelical Church as a whole. Will we love the world as God loves it? If we did develop that kind of heart for the world that in itself might significantly dampen the animosities and hatred many feel toward the citizens of the United States?

gather on the horizon. In that bleak moment in the life of our Lord, we find Jesus seeking out a place of prayer. During the most difficult and dark period in the life of Jesus, a time that the text describes as "agony," He goes to God the Father in "fervent" prayer. [15] Not only does He find a place of prayer during His time of testing, but also He encourages His disciples to do the same. Jesus knew the importance of prayer particularly during times of trial and testing. In this same Biblical account Jesus foresaw the abandonment His disciples would feel; He urged them to pray. Going to God when we face tragedy is a lesson this present generation of disciples would do well to learn. Consider the following passage from Luke 22: 39-44:

"And He came out and proceeded, as was His custom, to the Mount of Olives; and the disciples also followed Him. And when he arrived at the place, He had said to them, pray that you may not enter into temptation. And He withdrew form them about a stone's throw, and He knelt down and began to pray, saying, 'Father, if Thou art willing, remove this cup from Me; yet not My will, but Thine be done.' Now an angel from heaven appeared to Him, strengthening Him. And being in agony, He was praying fervently; and His sweat became like drops of blood, falling down upon the ground."

America -- September 11, 2001

Many churches around the country held special prayer services in the days immediately following the September 11, 2001, terrorist strikes on the United States. Those were uncertain days and people huddled together praying for help and courage. The Bible tells us in James 5:13, "Is anyone among you suffering? Let him pray." In the days and weeks following September 11th, it seemed that people all over the nation were willing to follow this directive.

I believe the Mount Scott Church in Oregon picked up on the overwhelming desire of people to find God in prayer immediately following the terrorist strikes on the United States. During their time of

---

[15] Luke 22:44

worship on September 16, they sang together a venerable hymn, *In the Garden* - a hymn about coming to the Lord in prayer.

During this time of crisis, there were prayers lifted for our national leaders, the President, the members of the Cabinet, members of Congress and the U.S. Armed Forces. Also there were prayers for those people living in Afghanistan, and other possible targeted areas in order that suffering and "collateral casualties" might be minimized. Prayers were also lifted for the perpetrators of these violent terrorist attacks. How beautifully they flowed from the lips of people of faith as they attempted to set aside their anger and fury in order to pray for those who had inflicted such an inhuman and hateful offence toward the people of this nation.

Prayers from the Week of September 11th

As you read the following prayers, consider lesson one. When you find yourself facing tragedy, pray. Also, pay careful attention to the petitions being lifted as we prepare to examine the second lesson or insight we gain from our study of the Church of God response to the September 11th terrorist strikes - what we pray for during times of tragedy.

"Father, right now we pray that You would be with everyone in the military... Lord, we pray that You would be with leadership right now... from Commander in Chief, our President, all the way down, that decisions would be made in the best interest of our country and the best interest of individual military members and their families. Lord, we pray that there would not be a rush to judgment, although justice is certainly what many of us want. Lord it's so hard sometimes to even identify what the problem is. Who did this? Really it's an ideology; it's a failure to turn to You. Lord, we pray that You would be with our country. It's a great country. We love our country, and we pray that You would keep everyone in our country safe, but particularly that You would be with service members as this plays out. Lord, there's a certainty that there are dangers for the military whether it is an overt or covert action, whether it just is in follow up terrorist

7

activities. We pray that You would be with them, and again Lord be with our leadership. And we are thankful for the faith of our current leader, and we pray that faith would permeate all down through the chain of command. Lord, help us always, not only as service members, but also as individuals to seek what Your will would be. Lord, we pray that You would be with our leaders and the military and that they would be seeking our will, not theirs... Keep them safe. Lord, we are thankful for them. In Your name we pray, Amen."[16]

Mitchell Burch
Vancouver First Church of God
Vancouver, Washington

"Our Father, we come before You in tears but with much thanksgiving. For we know that we serve a loving God, One who stands beside us in every trying situation, One who loves us when we do not understand the events that occur. Our Father, we especially thank You that we have seen multitudes turn and pray to God and ask for Your help in football stadiums, in churches, all nationalities, all ages...For, Lord, we know that our strength is in our Almighty God... Amen."[17]

Clyde Taylor
Towne Boulevard Church of God
Middletown, Ohio

"God, we do this morning, come before You. We lift up families that are grieving over lost loved ones; families that don't even know the status or whereabouts of loved ones. We lift them up to You. We also lift to You those firefighters, police officers and ordinary citizens that are scraping through the rubble searching for persons who may still be clinging to life. We lift them up to You at this hour. We also pray that we would not allow fear and anxiety and prejudice to overtake our hearts. We pray in Jesus' name. Amen."[18]

---

[16] Mitchell Burch. Special September 11th Prayer Service. Vancouver, Washington. September 11, 2001.

[17] September 16, 2001.

[18] September 16, 2001.

Jeff Mugford
Mountain Park Community Church
Phoenix, Arizona

"Heavenly Father, we come to You today. We are very grateful for our country; we are very grateful. You have placed us here. We understand, Lord, that the Word teaches us that we are supposed to pray for our leaders. Lord, often times when things are good, we ignore that [call.] We understand, Lord, that over the last several weeks, over the last month, it has been a critical time in our nation. These people gathered here in this assembly have been praying for our leaders, that You would give them wisdom and the patience to do exactly what You want them to do. Lord, we pray for our President and our Vice-President and each of the Cabinet members, members of Congress, each staff person, working on the issue in the military. Lord, we pray that Your Holy Spirit would hover around Afghanistan at this time. Lord, that You would be with our pilots, the U.N. workers on the ground, and the civilians. We also pray for our enemies. As someone said, 'We believe, Lord, in Your power to transform lives and to open eyes... We pray, Lord, that You would teach us to love those on the outside of our relational network; that our faith would be authentic and real; that we would be a conduit of the love of God, [a love] that loves not only those that are like us, those that please us, those that build us up, but those also, Lord, that are a challenge to us, that are different than we are, who do not see things the way we do, who do not worship the same 'God' that we worship. We pray, Lord, that we would be people of God and that Your power would flow through us."[19]

Gary Agee
Hopewell First Church of God
West Chester, Ohio

"Lord, we know that You have always been there for us. We humbly confess and repent for our nation that has taken You for

---

[19] October 14, 2001.

granted; that has so often enjoyed Your blessings without fulfilling the responsibilities of being a servant of God. Lord, we look to You and pray that You would have mercy upon us. Lord, that You would give us the protection that we need. For our security is not in the military. Our security is not in our governmental leaders. For, Lord, You have and are always the security that we need. You're our refuge and our strength. God, we pray You would protect us from any more terrorist activities that would seek to bring harm upon our nation and our land that, You would sovereignty rule and overrule in the activities of people. We pray humbly for Your protection. Father, we pray for the many churches that are gathered throughout this land today. Lord, be with the preachers and the ministers and those that share, that You would use them. For our service here today, we welcome You to be God, to minister to us. We pray for families that are grieving today that You would comfort them and give them hope and security and peace. Lord, bring a great ingathering during this time, that people would realize that they need You. Bless this service now. We pray this in Jesus' name. Amen."[20]

Mark Jackson
Towne Boulevard Church of God
Middletown, Ohio

John Spear made the following challenge to his congregation prior to praying the prayer that follows:

"You and I have joined together to pray for individuals in our nation who are in need of prayer. We are in need of prayer this day. I hope that we will continue to be a group of people called to prayer who will reach out to one another and to the people around the world through the power that God has given us through personal prayer to intercede for them, to lift them up, and to ask for God's special help in their incredible time of need.[21]

Lord Jesus, we thank You so much that You have made it possible for mankind to sing this song and many others like it

---

[20] September 16, 2001.
[21] John Spear. "Journey to the Heart of God." Casper, Wyoming. September 16, 2001.

10

which testify of the peace that comes to us in the midst of a terrible, terrible storm, peace that comes when our hearts are filled with anxiety or fear, peace that passes all understanding. The Scriptures teach us that we can have and know that we have a right standing with God. Thank you, this morning, for Your presence here in this worship service and worship services literally all over the world. Thank You for hearing our prayers, for ministering to those who need comfort, for those who need peace, those who need assurance and reassurance. Lord, may Your Spirit be loosed in such a way that this day would be exceedingly memorable in the heart of every worshipper as they gather together in churches and synagogues all around the world to lift up Your name, to pray for Your help, to ask for Your power to be unleashed. Thank You this morning for those of this assembly that we pray for, for answers to our prayers.... Thank you, Father, for teaching us, for opening up Your word, helping us, instructing us and guiding us through Your truth. Thank You Father, that there are many, many people today, who do not grieve as those who have no hope. Oh we wish, and we labor, and we pray that this kingdom of God would continue to expand, that hope would be deepened and broadened, that individuals would come to a saving knowledge of Jesus Christ, that God's forgiveness and God's hand would rest upon this nation and upon our world in such a way that people would see You and know Your love, and enter into a life changing relationship with You...a relationship that turns our hearts toward one another and away from evil, away from selfishness, away from independence. Lord we thank You for this opportunity to worship today. I pray that You would encourage every person here in this room through Your word, and through their own personal worship here today. Hear our prayer as we continue to worship You in Jesus' name." [22]

John Spear

---

[22] Ibid.

Heavenly Father, I simply want to say thank You for allowing us to be here right now in this moment, that we can reach out and touch, that we can feel the comfort and encouragement of our loved ones... not only in a physical family but [in our] church body... We think about those of our church family. Lord, we think about the thousands, the millions, affected by the tragedies this week that have occurred in New York, Washington D.C., and Pennsylvania, those families today that are separated from their loved ones, from wives, from husbands, aunts and uncles, grandparents and children, separated because of this tragedy. God, all we can do is ask right now that You would comfort them in their grief, and that there would be others around that would reach out and touch them to help them know that they are loved, that they are being prayed for and encouraged and helped even in this time of heartache. Lord, I think about our enemies who perpetrated this act. They need to know the love of God. They need to know Jesus Christ. They need to know that He can forgive. Lord, we are praying that they might discover Christ as their Savior. We're praying, Lord, that You would be with us; that we would be wise. We realize that justice is important. We realize that there are many actions that may be taken, politically and militarily. We know that those things may happen. We ask for Your wisdom that we will do what is appropriate, that we will do what is necessary, that ultimately in the end...not only will our country be strengthened but, Lord, overall may in some way the kingdom of God be lifted up as well. Please, Jesus, be with us. Strengthen us in this hour right here in this sanctuary. Amen."[23]

Robert Brink
Decatur Church of God
Decatur, Indiana

"Dear Lord, we stand this morning thanking You. Lord God, we stand this morning with adoration in our hearts. We adore You because

---

[23] September 16, 2001.

12

You are God all by Yourself. We adore You because You are a loving God. We adore You because You are a merciful God. As our country stands on the brink of war, and stands on the brink of so many things, people are finding out that they cannot make it without You. Lord God, we thank You that you show Yourself every time....First of all, we confess that we need You. We need You, Lord God, because You are all powerful. We need You, Lord God, because You know all things. And even when we can't understand what is going on, Lord God, Your purpose prevails. We confess to You that we are nothing but sinners who need a Savior. We thank You that you have saved us. Lord God, we thank You and we glorify You this morning. Oh Lord Jesus, we give You the glory and the praise...We pray for the leaders of this country. Lord God, we pray that Your hand would move mightily, and that we would move by your Spirit and not by vengeance...We ask that You would have Your way even in these times. Lord God, we pray that Your power would reign on the people of God, that they might see You...We know that people could lose their lives and that things could get unruly but...we are putting our trust in You... We put our hope in You. Oh Lord Jesus, we thank You this morning.... We pray for the children, who may be dealing with what they are seeing... We are praying for comfort, Lord God, in the name of Jesus. But in all things, we give You thanks; in all things; we give You glory. We will not let the devil [think] that we are defeated, because we have the victory in Jesus Christ. So we give You praise this morning, Lord... You said that if 'You be lifted up You would draw all men unto You.' We give You thanks this morning, Lord. We magnify You. We glorify You, Jesus. Have Your way. Have Your perfect way, Lord God, In the name of Jesus... Amen." [24]

Mark Richardson
Lincoln Avenue Church of God
Pittsburgh, Pennsylvania

"Oh Father, we pause to bless You, in the midst of our grief, to adore You. In the midst of heaviness in our hearts, we want to praise

---

[24] September 16, 2001.

You. Because, once again, we have been reminded that on, 'Christ the solid Rock we stand. And all other ground is sinking sand.[25]' We have been reminded Lord, that no matter what happens to us, those of us who know You have a refuge and strength, a very present help in times of trouble.[26] So, we want to come to thank You. Thank You for the gift of life. Thank You for the gift of mercy. Thank You for Your grace. Thank You for deliverance that we are not even aware of. Thank You, Lord, that You have been kind to so many of us. You have provided for us. You have comforted us this week. And we want to thank You, and we want to bless You... to submit to Your will and to let You know we are leaning on Your everlasting arms. 'What have I to dread, what have we to fear, leaning on the everlasting arms.'[27] Our hearts reach out, first of all, to our country. We pray for our country; we pray for our leaders, especially our President; for the members of Congress; and all the appointed officers who are in this country today. We pray that You will give them wisdom; that You'll give them understanding, that You will give them a sense of Your divine purpose and Your divine will. And even in the midst of all the discussions, the still small voice of God will be heard and followed. We commend our leaders to You. We ask You to protect and to guard them; to watch over them, to give them strength, energy and endurance. And we ask You to keep their ears and minds open to You. Bless our President. Keep Your hand upon him, Lord. Help him to keep on witnessing to the faith even in the midst of these crises. And, Lord, we pray for the city of New York. We pray for their leaders that You would give them endurance and courage. We pray for the firefighters and the rescue workers...that You would anoint them with fresh oil today. Give them fresh heavenly energy. Encourage them, Lord, even amidst the devastation and all the trauma with which they are dealing this morning; lift them to a higher plane. Encourage them as they serve and minister to those who are in need. And, Lord, our hearts reach out to those who are grieving this

---

[25] "The Solid Rock." Lyrics by Edward Mote and music by William B. Bradbury.

[26] Psalm 46: 1

[27] "Leaning on the Everlasting Arms." Lyrics by Elisha A. Hoffman and music by Anthony J. Showalter.

morning; fathers who have lost children, mothers who have lost children. Husbands have lost their wives; wives have lost their husbands. Men have lost friends, women have lost friends, and co-workers have been missing. God, I am praying that You will send the Holy Spirit who is Your Comforter, Your Guide and Your under girding power to hold them strong this morning. We don't know their names. But, God, it could have been us. We travel this road together. We reach out in faith, and we pray for them and we bless them; and we commend them to Your keeping, and we ask You, Lord, to minister to them. All over this country people are grieving. Wherever they are today, we ask You to visit them. And, Lord, we have this one prayer for ourselves, that You will teach us wisdom and give us a heart of wisdom, that You would 'help us number the days that we would get a heart of wisdom,' and that You may help us open our ears to what You are saying to us in this church, in this community, in this country, what You are saying about life, death and eternity. Help us to hear You. "Comfort Your people. Speak Ye comfort unto Your people"…Lift them up, this morning…And thank You that You have heard us, and that You are about to dispatch your angels to give grace and mercy. In Jesus name we ask it. Amen."[28]

Raymond Chin
Emerald Avenue Church of God
Chicago, Illinois

"Our Father and our God, we come to You today thankful that we can meet in Your name and in Your house. Our hearts are heavy from the events of this past week. God, we know that You are in control; that we are holding on to Your right hand. We not only have faith, but we trust in You, God, to get us through these difficult times. We pray for our leadership, and for our country, and for our people. Heal and mend us, God, this morning, but most of all we ask that You be with us in spirit and in deed this morning, so we can say it has been good and refreshing to be in Your house. Amen." [29]

---

[28] September 16, 2001.
[29] September 16, 2001.

Earl Wheatley, Jr.
North Park Church of God
Meridian, Mississippi

Larry Ortman made the following comments prior to leading his congregation in prayer:

"Will you bow your head and close your eyes? Pray to your Father about the evil in this world, this warped and diseased world that He sent His Son to die for [in order to] give life. Now, because of evil, cry out to the Lord for those people who have suffered so because of this tragedy. We need to pray for all those who are working to clear the debris to see if anyone could have survived. We need to pray for them and their safety. And let's pray for our President and his key staff, and so many other people who are in positions of leadership at this time, not only in our country but also around the world." [30]

"Our Father in heaven, we do our best to humble ourselves in Your presence. We have been unmistakably moved as we listened, and as we watched with shock and dismay at what was taking place just a few days ago. We don't understand; we don't know why; we cry out and say, 'Dear God, what can there be done in this world that You gave Your only Son to die for, [a world] that is so crooked, warped and diseased?' Out of that evil would raise this ugly head of destruction and devastation. God, as we have prayed for ourselves, and as we have prayed for children and students and adults alike, help us to recognize our responsibility to hold forth the Word of Life, to be a light in this evil, dark, diseased age…We humbly ask for comfort, for strength for those who have lost loved ones, for those who are trying to heal in a hospital somewhere back East, for families who are trying to understand how they are going to make it without their special loved ones…You call Yourself in Your Word 'the God of all comfort' and so, we are calling upon You to bring and give Your comfort, for ours falls so short. Father, this morning, we would pray for President Bush,

---

[30] Larry Ortman. "A Call to Prayer." Portland, Oregon. September 16, 2001.

16

Vice-President Chaney, and their administration. That as leaders, men and women alike, this would have shaken them to the core so they would cry out and say, 'I need to ask for wisdom from on high to be able to give leadership - just honest, righteous leadership.' When evil is present, how we wish to respond in ugly human ways. But we cry out for wisdom to know what justice would be like in this terrible, terrible mess. Bless those men and women, we ask. And as we humble ourselves before You, we ask that Your Holy Spirit would be able to move in the hearts of men and women starting with us right here, to bring light to this world, because Your light is so much greater and more powerful than darkness could ever be. Your love penetrates so much deeper and greater than the evil of this world could ever begin to penetrate. And so it is Your love, Your light, Your life that we ask for, and we pray for, and humble ourselves for. In the powerful name of Jesus Christ, this is our prayer." [31]

Larry Ortman
Mt. Scott Church
Portland, Oregon

After reading Psalm chapter five, Brad Sutter, from Anchorage, Alaska, introduced and then raised the following prayer:

"The Psalmist is a realist here, isn't he? There is trouble in the world. There is wickedness and, men do wicked things. But he ends that segment saying, 'but as for me I recognize God, that You are a God of loving kindness.' I am going to come to Your house and there at Your house, in reverence I am going to bow before Thee. We can do that today. We can do that today even in the wake of Tuesday morning...because the God of loving-kindness is here. He wants to hear our prayers. He wants to comfort our hearts. He is the solution to the problem that we have faced this week. So, let us look to Him in prayer as we begin this worship service."

"Great and mighty God, I thank You, Lord, that we can come this morning in reverence because of Your loving kindness, that we can come to worship You, that You have not changed today, that You are

---

[31] September 16, 2001.

the same as You were before Tuesday morning, You are the same God, still capable, still in control, God of loving kindness who does not delight in the wicked schemes of men. You are able to carry out Your plan even in the midst of this tragedy. Lord, it is to You our Rock that we come this morning. We want to worship You through song. We want to pour our hearts out to You in prayer, and we will do that Lord, later in this service as we hold up the needs of our country. Lord, we want to hear from Your Word today and let You speak to our hearts. So, Lord, we commit all of those things to You…In Jesus' Name. Amen." [32]

Brad Sutter
Cornerstone Church of God
Anchorage, Alaska

After affirming the sovereignty of God, Brad Sutter in this same service shared the following prayer:

"We would like to open the altars for prayer right now if you would like to come down to pray for someone, to pray for your country, to worship Him, whatever it may be. God's Word tells us to, 'be still and know that I am God.' God is not wringing his hands; He is in charge.

Heavenly Father, sovereign Lord of heaven and earth, we come to You now… You are the faithful God. You are the God of all power, of all wisdom. You are the God who knows the deepest recesses of every heart. Yet You are the God of infinite love, desiring to lavish that love upon us. Lord, we know that is true because, You have shown the perfect demonstration of that [love] through the sacrificial death of Your only begotten Son. So, we know that You love us. It is with that confidence that we come this morning in the midst of this tragedy in our country. We come boldly, Lord, before the very throne of Your grace in prayer to intercede this morning for our country. Lord, there are always many thousands and thousands of people experiencing tragedy every day…it has just been magnified [this week] due to such massive loss of life. Lord, we come to You with that

---

[32] Brad Sutter. Anchorage Alaska. September 16, 2001.

18

in the forefront of our minds, Lord, and we ask for Your grace, we ask for Your comfort… in the midst of those families who have lost loved ones. Oh God, would You do what only You can do? Through the Holy Spirit, the comforter as You called Him, we pray that You would reach into each one of those situations and that You would bring comfort as only You can do, that You would calm their hearts, Lord, and that You would give them hope in what appears to be a hopeless situation. Share Your love, Lord, with them. My primary prayer this morning is that if they do not know about Your love, and about what is available to them through the person of Jesus Christ, those individuals suffering loss would find that they would go from the ashes of death and destruction and would be resurrected to new life. We pray that would be true today. We pray that You would bring individuals around those that are suffering and those that are grieving, that could speak life and could speak hope into their hearts. Give Your people courage, Lord, I pray, that all across our country as people are questioning the meaning of life and how something like this could take place. That You would let the Christians with the message of hope, the message of peace, be courageous to speak that [hope] to their friends and to their neighbors…Lord, that you would take this tragedy and work it out for good…We ask, Lord, that your blessing would be upon this country in this time. God bless us with Your wisdom, and with Your presence, with the outpouring of Your Holy Spirit. I pray in Jesus Name." [33]

Brad Sutter
Cornerstone Church of God
Anchorage, Alaska

What We Pray

As we examine the above prayers, we gain a sense of the types of things for which pastors and leaders prayed when the citizens of this country were faced with the worst national tragedy in American history. By examining these petitions carefully, it is possible to gain some insight as to how one might pray through a personal tragedy.

---

[33] Ibid.

For what or for who do we pray when we find ourselves confronted with a personal tragedy?

Lesson 3: Thank God In Times Of Tragedy

Offering Thanks In Tragedy

One of the curious things we learn from an examination of the above prayers is that a number of them offered to the Lord thanksgiving even as they expressed heartfelt loss and grief at the tragic events of September 11, 2001. Pastor Chin thanked God for, "the gift of life, and for the gift of mercy." He thanked God for "deliverance" not immediately apparent through all the grief. John Spear from the Highland Park Church in Casper, Wyoming thanked the Lord for peace that comes in the midst of a "terrible, terrible storm." Earl Wheatley, Jr. of the North Park Church in Meridian, Mississippi, thanked God for the privilege of meeting in God's House. Though these expressions may seem out of place juxtaposed against the grief of a nation in mourning, they actually help us gain some much-needed perspective. Often times, when we experience a personal tragedy, we are unable to focus on anything other than our loss and the pain of that loss. Even in tragedy, we need to realize we are a blessed people. The perspective that produces this kind of gratefulness in the midst of tragedy allows that devastated couple whose child is born with a rare heart defect to appreciate the fact that their fragile baby was permitted to go home with them if only for the few days of its brief life. Or, the grieving family who has lost a grandpa would be able to somehow find the strength to offer thanks to God for his seventy-eight years of life on this earth. The writer of Ephesians tells us to use our tongues not for, "silly talk or course jesting," but rather, "giving of thanks." [34] In this same chapter, the writer gives the following instructions:

---

[34] Ephesians 5: 4

"And do not get drunk with wine, for that is dissipation, but be filled with the Spirit…always giving thanks for all things in the name of the Lord Jesus Christ to God, even the Father."[35]

The writer of Philippians says it this way:

"Be anxious for nothing, but in everything by prayer and supplication with thanksgiving let your requests be made known to God." [36]

By offering God thanks in the midst of tragedy, we are training our eyes to see the gracious and loving hand of God at work, despite the horror of the tragedy attempting to steer the pain and loss of the chaotic event in a positive redemptive direction, in short, turning the tragedy "hard to the right." As Paul addressing the believers in Rome confidently affirms:

"And we know that God causes all things to work together for good to those who love God, to those who are called according to His purpose." [37]

Lesson 4: Pray And Commit To Making Necessary Changes As You Face Tragedy

A Prayer Of Repentance

In the story of Jonah, we find that the tragedy he faced, death by drowning in a raging ocean after being tossed overboard, was one of his own making. He had deliberately disobeyed the Lord by refusing to go to Nineveh to preach. In the wake of the September 11th terrorist strikes, there was a sense in the minds of a number of ministers across the country that a prayer of repentance was in order. Mark Jackson from Middletown, Ohio, picked up on this theme, praying that we in this nation would be forgiven, "For we have enjoyed the blessings of God without fulfilling the responsibilities."[38] Tom Howland remarked

---

[35] Ephesians 5:18-20

[36] Philippians 4: 6

[37] Romans 8:28

[38] Mark Jackson. Middletown, Ohio. September 16, 2001.

that, "Our nation was experiencing what any nation that forgets God experiences."[39]

Dr. Timothy Clarke in his sermon on Sunday, September 16th, stated that America had "broken God's heart."[40] Paul Sheppard, speaking to his congregation on Sunday, September 16th, suggested that America was guilty of inviting God out of its national life." [41]

Often times, individuals make decisions that are unwise. These misguided decisions cause unspeakable grief. For example, a person chooses to drive under the influence, or chooses to be unfaithful to a spouse or chooses to do violence against another person. In each of these cases,   people have created their own tragedies simply because of misguided thinking . When we face a tragedy of our own making, it is appropriate for us to turn to God and to admit our sin, and then to leave that attitude, behavior, or habit in our past – genuinely quit it. Sometimes, it is the sin of omission that leads to the making of a personal tragedy; something that we have not done which brings us great grief and pain. In either case, a prayer of repentance is appropriate.

Lesson 5: Pray For The Victims Of Tragedy

When the citizens of this nation realized on the morning of September 11, 2001 that our country was under attack, prayers were raised in every city across the United States. It seemed instinctive to pray for those immediately affected by the tragedy. There were, of course, prayers for those trapped in the doomed World Trade Center Towers, those missing in the Pentagon and those killed on the hijacked airliners. There were prayers for the thousands of people walking from hospital to hospital in hopes of finding a lost loved one. There were prayers for those who may have been trapped alive by the falling debris and the families of those lost in the tragedy. Following the

---

[39] Tom Howland. "What Are We Going To Do Now?" Andover, Kansas. September 16, 2001.

[40] Dr. Timothy Clarke. "A Word of Hope." Columbus, Ohio. September 16, 2001.

[41] Paul Sheppard. "An American Tragedy." Menlo Park, California. September 16, 2001.

attacks, a new sense of the importance of praying for people in distant cities was born, in a way that people sitting comfortably in North American congregations had not experienced in many years. Perhaps, one of the critical lessons learned from the September 11th terrorist attacks was that we are, in fact, "one nation under God." If calamity strikes a distant city, it is the responsibility of Christians all over this nation to lift up the victims in prayer. The sweet national unity in which the citizens of this nation reveled following the September 11th terrorist strikes, may have been a direct result of the many voices united in prayer for those who suffered so profoundly.

Lesson 6: Remember To Pray For National And Local Leaders

The Scriptures teach us that we are to pray for those in authority so that we may live in peace. Consider the Apostle Paul's instructions to his understudy, Timothy:

"First of all, then, I urge that entreaties and prayers, petitions and thanksgivings, be made on behalf of all men, for kings and all who are in authority, in order that we may lead a tranquil and quiet life in all godliness and dignity. This is good and acceptable in the sight of God our Savior." [42]

Far too often, the above directive is ignored until times of national tragedy. However, as is apparent, in the above-recorded prayers, these Biblical instructions were taken to heart immediately following the September 11th attacks on the United States of America. It was as if citizens all across this nation inside and outside the church realized that our President and his cabinet, the military commanders, the foreign diplomats, and the military units on the ground were in desperate need of our prayers. Prayers were raised for fire and rescue workers, law enforcements agencies, and even teachers whose task it would be to try to bring help and comfort to their students. At this critical time in our nation's history, we learned once again the importance of praying for our leaders and our public servants.

---

[42] I Timothy 2:1-3

I Timothy 2:1-3 points out that God wants us to pray for those in authority so our lives could be led in peace. How much of the personal tragedies that we face in our cities or neighborhoods could be averted if we would pray specifically for national, state, and local leaders? It not only moves the hand of God, but it changes our perspective of our role in the community. It is as if the problems in our nation, state, and community become our challenges. When we pray in this manner, we often find ourselves in a position to help make our communities better places to live, work, and worship.

It is interesting also to note that, *God Bless America*, became the patriotic anthem of choice immediately following the tragic events of September 11th. It seemed everyone was singing it. A great many churches that were surveyed for this book sang *God Bless America* in their morning worship services the weekend of September 16, 2001. The lyrics of the song compose a prayer for God's blessing on this nation, a blessing people all over this country craved following the horrors of September 11th.

Lesson 7: Pray For Courage

During this crisis, a unique atmosphere of fear pervaded our nation.

Terry Ball from Monroe, Ohio, described it this way, "The events of this week have made us all wonder, and made us afraid." [43]

Greg Smith from Birmingham, Alabama, echoed this sentiment: "As the dust settled literally, and as time passed, and as the full ramifications of this thing sank in, and as our response began to become more evident, I tell you, in my own heart and in my own life, I began to feel an overwhelming sense of fear, like I have never before felt. Is it safe to travel? Can I trust anyone who doesn't look just like me? Where will they hit again? We live pretty close to Atlanta....What

---

[43] Terry Ball. "The Soul..." Monroe, Ohio. September 16, 2001.

if these guys get a hold of some anthrax? What about biological warfare? What about the well- being of my daughters?"[44]

My two sons, younger brother and I visited Ground Zero over the Christmas break about three and a half months after the September 11th terrorist strikes. As we were walking near the site, we noticed a large banner with praying hands hanging from one of the nearby buildings. The banner had been placed there by the United Methodist Church. It read, "Fear is not the only force at work in the World today." I found this banner very encouraging. Prayer was a powerful way of battling the terror that many of the citizens of this nation were facing in the wake of the September 11th strikes; a terror that this nation had not experienced in at least a generation. Throughout the days and weeks following the September 11th terrorist strikes, we prayed that God would give us courage.

Just as this national tragedy brought a certain level of fear to this nation, personal tragedy also has a tendency to evoke a suffocating fear in the lives of all who experience it up close and personal. When a woman who has been married for decades suddenly has to face life alone, fear and uncertainty rush in like a flood. She wonders, will I be able to take care of myself? Who will be here to protect me? Who will care for me when I am old? The person battling illness wrestles with profound questions that evoke primal fears. Do I have cancer? Am I going to die? What will come of my children?

In Scripture, we find that over and over again God's people called on Him when they were afraid. God answered these prayers and took care of His people. Frequently in the New Testament, the Lord tells his followers, "Do not be afraid." When we find ourselves facing personal tragedy, we pray, as people across our nation did on September 11th, confident that His courage will be born in us. A courage that allows us to live in peace no matter what the nature of the tragedy we might be facing.

---

[44] Greg Smith. Birmingham, Alabama. September 16, 2001.

Lesson 8: During Times Of Tragedy,
Pray For Your Enemies

Not long after the terrorist strikes of September 11th, I attended a ministers' meeting in which as a group we gathered to pray. During this special time of prayer, we were to pray for the many concerns surrounding this unprecedented national crisis. We prayed for many different groups of people: the victims, the rescue workers, the President, and the Congress. To my surprise, however, we did not pray for our enemies. I am convinced this was simply an oversight. Having said this, it should be noted that prayer for one's enemies was perhaps the most critical part of any prayer raised following the September 11th strikes on the United States. For, in our prayers for our President, the rescue workers, and the victims of the terrorist attacks, we were praying, in a way, for "our people." Jesus, on the other hand, taught us to love the "other," the one who is not like us, the one on the outside of our relational network, our enemy. Consider His immortal words: "You have heard that it was said, 'You shall love your neighbor, and hate your enemy.' But I say to you, love your enemies, and pray for those who persecute you."[45]

One of the most peace-loving things an individual can do when they find that they have an enemy is to pray for that person. It is simply impossible to sincerely bring a person to the Lord in prayer without walking away with a whole new view of that person - a more God-centered, compassionate view.

Consider the prayer voiced by the Barry Shafer from Middletown, Ohio:

"Lord, it is in obedience to Your Word that we pray for our enemies. Father, lift the veil of deception that they have accepted. May they see the truth? It can happen, Lord. It can happen. And, Lord, we have total confidence in Your Spirit and Your ability and power to transform lives. Lord, maybe this is the peace that everyone is praying

---

[45] Matthew 5:43-44

for; maybe this is the unity that Jesus prayed for. Maybe that is what we are on the brink of when we lift up our enemies."[46]

As we consider how praying for our enemies might help us to cope with personal tragedy, please consider the fact that the hateful scheming of the Al Qaida network of terrorists operating from Afghanistan and self-proclaimed enemies of this nation were believed to be responsible for the national tragedy of September 11th.

By praying for these people, we want for them to repent, to turn to God, and for God to work in a redemptive way to forgive and have mercy on them. Having said that, it is not to say that we wanted the perpetrators of this heinous act to go unpunished. God is a God of justice, and we want justice to be done. God is loving, yes, but He is not indifferent to those whose lives were inhumanly sacrificed on September 11th. When one of His people harms another, He certainly will right that wrong either now or in eternity.[47]

Many of the tragedies people find themselves in today, are the result of one person hurting another, sometimes intentionally. A spouse breaks his or her marriage vows, leaving the victim spouse with the kids and the broken pieces. The temptation is to allow anger and bitterness to take up residence. Also a pastor can grieve as a result of being wronged by a member of his or her church. The lesson of September 11th regarding praying for one's enemies applies in both situations. We are to pray for the one who we have labeled an enemy. I would argue that if they have a belly button, then they are not really

---

[46] "911, God, God are You There?" Middletown, Ohio. September 16, 2001.

[47] I understand the demands of justice are ultimately met in the crucifixion of Jesus. I think what we often mistakenly call forgiveness is merely apathy. We as casual observers looking into the lives of the families of the victims don't care about the victim enough to demand that justice be done. Justice is not a job for the squeamish. The servant of the Lord does not carry the sword in vain according to the Apostle Paul. It is relatively easy for me as a pastor to tell the parents of a murdered child to forgive the perpetrator. Obviously, I can't value the child as the parents do. Justice is done only when both the life of the victim and the perpetrator are fully appreciated at the most fundamental level. When the scale is tipped in favor of either the victim or the perpetrator or when either of these lives are elevated one over the other, injustice abides, and God's will has not been done.

the enemy. By praying for the perpetrator we begin to secure God's compassion for them. We see them from God's perspective, as wayward children. In this healthy spiritual climate, it then becomes possible to despise the sin in the life of the person and at the same time love the sinner. This compassionate attitude is an essential part of getting through tragedy. Directing hate toward an individual who has wronged you, will not allow you to heal.

Lesson 9: When You Face Tragedy, You May Find Help By Praying The Lord's Prayer

Todd Beamer, one of the heroes of Flight 93, which crashed in western Pennsylvania on September 11th, prayed the Lord's Prayer with Lisa Jefferson, a supervisor with the GTE Customer Center. Immediately following the prayer, a courageous group of passengers on the ill-fated flight intentionally foiled the hijacking and crashed the jet into a field near the town of Shanksville, Pennsylvania. Their actions saved the lives of who knows how many on the ground. The Hamilton First Church of God in Hamilton, Ohio, prayed the Lord's Prayer during their morning worship time the Sunday after the terrorist strikes. The North Anderson Church in Anderson, Indiana also prayed this Lord's Prayer together during the worship service on that same morning.

Other pastors and churches looked to the prayer that the Lord taught his disciples during those uncertain days following the September 11th terrorist attacks in an attempt to bring their concerns to the Lord and to find some measure of peace. I emphasized a couple of phrases in the Lord's Prayer in my own message delivered Sunday morning September 16th.

On September 11th, I was to attend a scheduled district ministers' meeting. On the afternoon of that fateful day, I was to attend a small group training session with my key church leaders. Despite the horrific news of September 11th, a decision was made to go on with the regularly scheduled events of the day. I must admit it was hard to stay focused on the agenda items covered in that meeting. As my mind wandered, I noticed that the walls of the meeting room were bare with

28

the exception of a solitary plaque inscribed with the words of the Lord's Prayer. I thought about the words of this prayer the Lord taught his disciples to pray in the uncertain days of his own earthly ministry. Following this ministers' meeting I met my leaders in the sanctuary for the afternoon workshop. Before the scheduled video presentation, we gathered in small groups to pray for the events surrounding the September 11th terrorist strikes. One of my church leaders spontaneously led our group in the immortal words of the Lord's Prayer. I wondered later, what was the appeal of this prayer, in that desperate moment in time. I made the following comments about some of the petitions in Lord's Prayer in my sermon delivered on the Sunday after the terrorist strikes.

God, "Our Father"

"God has more kids than just us...He is Everyone's father...At times like this, we can pray this prayer thinking that God will only take care of us. We need to understand, God has more kids than just us...This will help us to mature as believers...If we really begin to think this way, perhaps we would then pay a little more attention to what is going on around the world, when there is a famine in Africa, or when there is trouble in Malaysia. God has a big family...we should not be indifferent to the needs and hurts of people around the world...If we took on that kind of mentality, then maybe the animosity towards this country would not be so great." [48]

Thy Kingdom Come

"Maybe what is attractive about this prayer is that we pray, 'Thy kingdom come.' Now, to our relatively tranquil country, violence has come. Maybe now we sense with urgency that we want God's kingdom to be here. When it comes, there will be a reign where there is ever-increasing love and toleration for others. We won't have to worry about nuclear attacks, biological weapons, terrorist attacks, or

---

[48] Gary Agee. "Tragedy and Triumph." West Chester, Ohio. September 16, 2001.

chemical weapons being used. When God's kingdom comes, we won't have to worry about violence of one toward the other. It is that place where God is in charge, and God reigns, and people act like God's children. We long for that place where the 'lion and the lamb' lie down together in peace; where God reigns. Where differences of cultures do not lead to these types of acts of violence. We are asking, then, when we pray for God's reign to spread, that it would spread to our lives and to the lives of the people that we love. Expand, Oh kingdom; expand and swallow us up!" [49]

Deliver Us From Evil

"Maybe what is appealing about the Lord's Prayer is the passage, 'Deliver us from evil.' We have seen evil in all of its ugliness. We understand, though, that evil is rebellion against the Lord. I like what the President said. He said, 'We are on a campaign to rid evil from the world.' Now, that is pretty ambitious. We understand that evil in this setting took on the form of planes crashing into buildings, used like missiles. However, we also need to understand that evil is a problem here in our lives. Evil is greed, the habit of making all we can and being selfish. It is caring only about the individual, myself, me, me, me. This leads to terrible consequences. Greed, indifference, pride, prejudice, and lust -- all of us have these to a greater or lesser degree. If we are going to rid the world of evil, let us start with us. Let us pull the proverbial telephone pole out of our own eye, so that we can see clearly to remove the speck in our brother's eye. It starts with having the Lord forgive us of our sins and walking in the light. It starts by understanding what the Lord's will is for our lives, and obeying, obeying, obeying what the Lord tells us to do." [50]

Lesson 10: Remember During Times of Tragedy, That God Answers Our Prayers

---

[49] Ibid.
[50] Ibid.

In the story of Jonah, he was disobedient to his call and ended up in the ocean during a fierce storm. Jonah 2:1 says, "Then Jonah prayed." If you find yourself in trouble, facing a horrible, personal tragedy in your own life, or if you don't think you even have the strength to finish the day, let alone tomorrow- pray. Would God answer the prayers of the person whose wounds are self-inflicted? According to the book of Jonah, the amazing, wonderful answer is "Yes." Chapter 2, verse 2 says, "I called out of my distress to the Lord, and He answered me. I cried for help from the depth of Sheol; thou didst hear my voice."

Consider the words of the Psalmist in Psalm 28:6. "Blessed be the Lord God because He has heard the voice of my supplication." Again in Psalm 34:1-2, 4: "I will bless the Lord at all times; His praise shall continually be in my mouth. My soul shall make its boast in the Lord. The humble shall hear it and rejoice...I sought the Lord and He answered me, And He delivered me from all my fears." The writer of the book of James gives us confidence that man can accomplish much through prayer.

He writes, "The effective prayer of a righteous man can accomplish much." [51]

In the introduction and chapter one, we looked at ten lessons or insights we can gain from an examination of the response of the Church of God Reformation Movement to the events of September 11th. Now that we have completed our study of prayer, let's move on to chapter two, where we will examine how we can persevere through personal tragedy by proclaiming God's presence in our lives and professing His power over all the forces that come against us.

---

[51] James 5:16

Chapter One Questions for Discussion

1.) How did the events of September 11th impact your prayer life?

2.) Were you able to pray for your enemies immediately following the strike on the United States?

3.) Have the events of September 11th helped you realize the need to pray for our President and the government of our nation? Explain.

4.) Skim over the prayers recorded in this chapter. In what ways are your prayers you prayed following the terrorist strikes of September 11th similar? In what ways are the prayers you lifted different?

5.) What is it about experiencing tragedy that makes us more urgent in our prayer life?

6.) Discuss a time in your life when your prayers were passionate and you called to the Lord with "all of your heart."

7.) Are you praying for your enemies? How do you think that might affect the way you feel about them?

Chapter Two
Presence And Power

"I am so grateful for My Beloved. The things that catch us by surprise do not catch God by surprise because, long before anything happens, He already knows."

Dr. Rita Johnson.
Sumpter Community Church of God
Belleville, Michigan

"I think the ultimate question is, 'On Tuesday, when all of this was taking place, was, where was God?' Was He simply sitting on His hands? God offers insights in His Book that He has given to us. There are many words in the Bible that can offer us hope and encouragement, I believe this morning, that God wants me to deliver a message that allows all of us to restore our hope in Him and to be encouraged in knowing that He is God supreme, and that He still rules on this earth."

Paul Mumaw
First Church of God
St. Joseph Michigan

"Where is our God? People, I know that there are tragedies out there. I know that there are heartaches that we sometimes experience. But there is hope. There is help. There is Jesus… I want us to join together in believing that we can turn tragedy into triumph…But I know, even as our country is professing today, that when there seems to be no other hope, when there seems to be no other help available, God is still here."

Robert Brink
Decatur Church of God
Decatur, Indiana

"God is still in charge. Regardless of what people are saying, regardless of what people may be planning, God is still in charge."

Don Bethany
New Testament Church of God
Brooklyn, New York

"God is constant...He is constantly in our presence; He is constantly working in our midst...He is constantly there for you and for me...God is not sunk. No matter what the devastation, no matter what kind of tragedy that has befallen this place, please know that God is constant."

Rolland Daniels
Salem Church of God
Clayton, Ohio

Lesson 11: During Times Of Tragedy, Proclaim God's Presence

September 11, 2001, was in many ways America's darkest day. An estimated 3,056 people were killed on crashing planes and in collapsing buildings in New York, Washington, D.C., and in a field near Shanksville, Pennsylvania.[52] Many people in this nation wanted to know, following the violent attacks of September 11th, that God had not abandoned us in our country's greatest hour of need. Would He be with us as we were forced to transverse during those dark days "the valley of the shadow of death?"

In the New Testament, we find Jesus and his disciples in a similar desperate situation. It was the darkest hour of Jesus' life. He had just celebrated the Passover meal with His disciples, and with foreboding He waited for His own impending death. While He waited, He attempted to prepare His sometimes-timid followers for His coming arrest and crucifixion. On that dark night, as He shared with His closest followers that He was going to be returning to the Father, He could see the confusion and pain in their faces. They had walked with Him, they had believed, sometimes imperfectly, His words, and they had abandoned their former lives to preach the Lord's message of love.

---

[52] USA Today, 30 May, 2002.

Now their Lord, their mentor and friend was leaving them to fend for themselves. What kind of hope could He offer His disciples as they contemplated life without Him? It was following the Passover meal that He made the following promise in order to steady their aching souls.

"And I will ask the Father and He will give you another Helper, that He may be with you forever; that is the Spirit of truth, whom the world cannot receive, because it does not behold Him or know Him, but you know Him because He abides with you, and will be in you. I will not leave you as orphans; I will come to you."[53]

How these words, a promise that His presence would always be with them in the future, must have softened the devastating announcement of His departure.

Following the tragic events of September 11th, many across the nation found some comfort in the words of Psalm 46 quoted in pulpits all across the country. A number of churches across America had this psalm read during their Sunday services on September 16th. As one examines this psalm, it is easy to see why these ancient words were such a source of inspiration and encouragement during the uncertain days of that dark time.

"God is our refuge and strength, a very present help in trouble. Therefore we will not fear though the earth should change, and though the mountains slip into the heart of the sea; Though its waters roar and foam, though the mountains quake at its swelling pride. There is a river whose streams make glad the city of God, the holy dwelling places of the Most High. God is in the midst of her, she will not be moved; God will help her when morning dawns. The nations made an uproar, the kingdoms tottered; He raised His voice, the earth melted. The Lord of hosts is with us; The God of Jacob is our stronghold. Come, behold the works of the Lord, who has wrought desolations in the earth. He makes wars to cease to the end of the earth; He breaks the bow and cuts the spear in two; He burns the chariots with fire. 'Cease striving and know that I am God; I will be exalted among the

---

[53] John 14:16-18

nations, I will be exalted in the earth.' The Lord of hosts is with us; the God of Jacob is our stronghold."[54]

Perhaps, the most important reason why this psalm seemed to offer so much hope for people following the September 11th terrorist strikes is that, at least for God's people, it contains the promise of God's presence even in the midst of earth-shattering tragedy and almost unimaginable geologic upheaval. The above psalm makes at least three references to the presence of God in spite of the incredible tumultuous events described in verses two and three. In verses one, seven, and eleven, the promise of God's presence in the lives of His people is abundantly clear. This same promise helped to steady us when, after the events of September 11th, our foundation of security and safety began to "quake."

Paul Dreger from Goshen, Indiana, shared this truth with his congregation on the Sunday after the terrorist strikes:

"Psalm 46 reminds us that no matter what comes our way, God is with us. God is here. God was at the World Trade Center on Tuesday morning. God was at the Pentagon on Tuesday morning. God was at home all across the country, even around the world. There were hundreds of foreigners in the World Trade Center Tuesday morning. Let's not forget this. This was an act of terror against the world, not just against America. All around the world, where homes were in turmoil, God was there." [55]

In many of the sermons delivered across the country on the Sunday following the September 11th terrorist strikes, pastors found themselves attempting to answer the question, "Where was God on September 11th?"

From my own pulpit, I addressed this difficult question as follows:

"Where was God in all of this? Well, God was present. Our merciful Father was present. Our merciful Father was present when the

---

[54] Psalm 46:1-11

[55] Paul Dreger. Goshen, Indiana. September 16, 2001.

36

[planes] were exploding. Our merciful Father was present when the cell phones were ringing, giving those final salutations. Our God was present as the horror of death neared for those on the plane…God was already present, taking this horrible violent act and turning it, turning it, turning it toward the good." [56]

In his message delivered on September 16th from his pulpit in Indianapolis, Indiana, Dr. G. David Cox considered straying from his scheduled series of messages on the life of Joseph. As he contemplated this decision, however, he reread Genesis 39:2. This passage affirms God's presence in the life of Joseph, even though the young man had just experienced perhaps the worst possible tragedy he could have imagined: separation from his beloved father and family, loss of freedom, and the strangeness of a foreign land. Dr. Cox discusses his decision to continue his series on Joseph in the Sunday, September 16th worship service:

"When I saw those words in this text, I said, 'I will continue the series,' because if God could be with Joseph in the darkest hour of his life, He will be with us in our dark hour. If God could prosper Joseph down there as a slave in the land of Egypt, He can prosper us in all of our brokenness as His people today."[57]

Robert Brink, from Decatur, Indiana, shared the following:

"Saturday morning, I was able to catch just a little bit of the children being interviewed on two different stations … I heard those questions asked, 'Where is God?' 'Where is God in this?'…Where is God when you have Joseph, just one of twelve brothers…loved certainly by his dad, probably favored by his dad …It wasn't an enemy that did him in. It wasn't somebody that was a neighbor that was angry that came across and punished him. His own brothers, ten of his brothers, took him and sold him into slavery. He was carried off to Egypt. Carried off to a foreign land. And you might want to say,

---

[56] Gary Agee. "Tragedy and Triumph." West Chester, Ohio. September 16, 2001.

[57] Dr. G. David Cox. "The Life of Joseph." Indianapolis, Indiana. September 16, 2001.

37

'Where is your God, Joseph?' And Joseph gets out of slavery then starts to rise up. He's now become a servant in the home of Potipher, one of the Egyptian leaders. He is rising in stature within the home. He becomes basically the head servant. He is in charge of all of the servants. He is in charge of all of the household activities…He seems to be blessed a little bit in the midst of his slavery. Then Potipher's wife falsely accuses him of pursuing her, and Joseph is put into prison. Where is your God, Joseph? Joseph is in prison and then, because of the spiritual gift of being able to interpret dreams, he has two servants of the Pharaoh who are put in prison with him. And they have dreams. He explains their dreams to them. One of them is the chief butler… who is going to return to his position as part of his dream. Joseph says, 'When you get there would you tell Pharaoh about me?' And the butler is restored… He gets back to Pharaoh and you know what he does? He forgets all about Joseph. Joseph, where is your God? Shadrach, Meshach, and Abednego lived in a land that was overrun by an enemy…you want to say, 'Well, where is your God?' But God did give them an opportunity, even in this foreign land to become leaders. They were trained to rise up and become leaders in this new land…This King Nebuchadnezzar really thought a lot of himself. So much so, that he built a huge statue of himself …[and] everyone was to bow down and worship him, because he considered himself a god. He had such a high opinion of himself… and he commanded all of the people, not only the political officials, but all of the people when they heard…. the sound of the trumpet, to bow down, and they were to worship the idol, the statue, their god, Nebuchadnezzar. Shadrach, Meshach, and Abednego said, 'We couldn't do that…' They knew they couldn't do that, so they were thrown into the fiery furnace. Shadrach, Meshach, and Abednego, where is your God? …The apostle Paul had this tremendous experience where he saw Christ on the Damascus Road, and because of it, he became a Christian - a believer in the kingdom of God. In the process of serving God, he was at one point, stoned. I mean he was taken out and he was beaten by a mob; they literally took stones and threw at him to kill him. They left him in the street as dead. Paul later, because he was being faithful and doing everything he was supposed to…was placed into prison for a number of years in Caesarea, where he dwelt because the king of that area…kept thinking that Paul might buy his way out of prison; in other words, bribe him to let Paul go. He was in prison for a number of years. Paul, where is your God? … On the way to Rome, Paul is shipwrecked and cast up on the shore. Paul, where is your God? If we were to quit right now, it would be pretty discouraging… Where is our God? Abraham was up on the mountain with his son Isaac. He had him tied up, [he] had the knife poised and was ready to offer him as a sacrifice [because] he believed he was supposed to. God was there, providing a ram in the bushes so that ram would be offered instead of his son. Where is God? Moses found him in a burning bush [when] a voice came to him out of the midst of a bush, 'Take off your sandals, Moses, you are on holy ground.' Where is God? Samuel was in his bedroom when he heard, 'Samuel, Samuel.' God was speaking to him. It took him a while to understand because he was young… Elijah found God on a mountaintop, when God responded to his prayers and sent fire, which consumed an offering [with such] a powerful manifestation of God's presence, that the prophets of Baal were then destroyed. Where is our God? Jonah found him in the belly of a great fish… Where is our God? Bartimaus found him on the side of the road when he called out to Jesus, and Jesus healed his eyes and made him well. Where is our God? Lazarus found him when he was called off of a slab lying in a tomb dead. Lazarus was awakened, got up, and had to step outside the tomb to confront his Jesus who was outside calling him out. Where is our God? Stephen was in the street and the stones were coming at him. They were hitting his body, killing him, actually killing him. And he saw his God sitting on a throne, sitting on the throne waiting for him to come home. Where is our God? I want you to know that John the revelator saw Him coming again in a vision. Where is our God? He is there. He is here. He is all about us. Tragedy will come no doubt. Because sin came into our world, evil entered it, and it became a part of the world we live in. That will not change as long as we live in this world. So, the pain is there and it is going to be. The hurt is there, and it is going to be. But we can get through it. That is the promise. I say sometimes it means we will live through [the hurt.] Sometimes it means we are going to glory through [the pain.]...But we know that we have a God that has prepared a place for us. He said, 'I have prepared a place for you and I will return.' He is not going to leave us. He is not going to forsake us." [58]

In his message on Sunday, September 23rd, Greg Smith from Birmingham, Alabama, shared the following comforting story, which illustrates how God is always present, and watches over His people:

"I have told you this story before, but it bears repeating, of a young Indian brave who was about twelve years of age and was entering into his passage into manhood. There was a ceremony that was devised by the tribe. A right of passage would take place for any young man at this point in his life. After an elaborate ceremony around the fire with the tribe, the young man would be given just a knife. He [was then] sent out into the wilderness by himself with no other form of protection or provision. He was instructed to cut wood, to build a fire, to kill game, and to spend the entire night alone all on his own. The night was dark and long, and the young brave slept very little, even the slightest noise, caused his skin to crawl. Just as the sun was beginning to rise, the young brave woke with a start, for he had heard the snapping of twigs behind him. He instinctively grabbed his knife, cautiously lifted his head, and silently stood to his feet. He peered out beyond the immediate brush. There to his surprise stood his father, bow in arrow in hand. He had been there all night watching over his son, knowing what was around him; knowing what was taking place; knowing that, even though the young brave did not know it, the father was still in control. God knows. That is how God is with us." [59]

He continued:

"There will be times when confusion will occur. There will be times when our leaders, because they are human, are going to make mistakes. We are aware that this conflict is not going to be brief but, through it all, God says to us today, as He said to Joshua long ago, 'Be strong and courageous. Do not be terrified; do not be discouraged for

---

[58] Robert Brink. Decatur, Indiana. September 16, 2001.
[59] Greg Smith. Birmingham, Alabama. September 23, 2001.

the Lord your God is with you wherever you go.' Our God is an awesome God. He brings hope. We don't know what will happen tomorrow or the next day, but we do know who is with us. I urge you to be strong and take heart, to place your confidence in Him, the God who will never leave us, the God who will never forsake us." [60]

Steve Carney from Morehead, Kentucky, said it this way:
"God is at my right hand that I may not be shaken. He is at my right hand; I don't have to be shaken.' What's going on and why? The Lord is with me. He is right here beside me. Did you ever feel the comfort of having someone you love right there beside you? That's so important and so precious, because, in a tough time, the comfort that you receive from somebody being there makes a big difference in your life. Not everybody can be there. I remember one time I was going through a difficult time in my life and I decided I was going to go for a walk. I don't know why she did this, but Amanda [his daughter] left her homework and decided to walk with me. She came up beside me and just kind of put her arm in my arm. I was going through a tough time inwardly. I was just so comforted by her nearness, and I looked at her and said, "Amanda, you're a comfort for your old father's heart." And she looked at me and said, "You are to mine."…. Think of the comfort in your life. If you are in prayer and worshipping the Lord, and beholding Him in your presence, behold Him until you can see Him at your right hand. He's at my right hand. If you could see Him, if you knew nothing stood between you and Him, if you never allowed a sin, if you never allowed a sorrow, or a heartache to keep you from Him, what comfort would that bring to your soul? But you always would bring it all into His presence, I mean always… If you would bring yourself to a place, a holy walk with the Lord, a walk where you've got Jesus right there beside you, you're not going to let anything stand between you and Him…. Then, my friends, you are going to fear nothing; you know that you're all right, because you've got the God of heaven and earth; you've got Jesus Christ risen from the dead at your right hand; you've got the one that can comfort your

---

[60] Ibid.

heart, the one that can let you know, that He can take care of you. [Jesus said,] 'I am with you always even to the end of the world.' If you've got the one who created the heavens and the earth walking beside you, if God be with you, who can stand against you? No one."[61]

Carl Addison from Sikeston, Missouri, in his September 16th message on the Stoning of Stephen, declares both the power and presence of the sovereign God at work despite the evil perpetrated by the terrorists on Tuesday, September 11th. He offered his congregation the following words of encouragement:

"First of all, when we are attacked, God is still with us…as in the passage of Scripture we read about Stephen; you have to see this. In verse fifty-five it says, 'But Stephen, full of the Holy Spirit, looked up to heaven and he saw the glory of God and Jesus standing at the right hand of God.' He said, 'Look! I see heaven opened and the Son of Man standing at the right hand of God." In the midst of the attack, in the midst of what he was going through, God made himself known to Stephen. He let him have a glimpse of Himself. What we learn by this is that, no matter how dark and horrendous the attack is, no matter how difficult the struggle is, no matter what it is we are living for, no matter how evil and dark the days are, when we are under attack, God is still with us. Now, this is crucial to understand because it didn't feel like that Tuesday. Maybe your attack today is something other than what we are living through as a nation but, when we are under siege or when things get dark, it seems like God is no longer there. There is a great Psalm in the Old Testament. It is the 46th Psalm. It addresses that very feeling, the feeling that God is no longer present. The Psalmist writes and he says, 'God is our refuge and strength, an ever present help in trouble.' Don't you love that phrase? 'Ever present.' What he means by that is that there isn't ever a time when He is [absent.] He is always present. He is constantly present. So, in those moments when we are under attack, God didn't change. You see here is the thing, Tuesday everything changed except God. He is still the same, and He

---

[61] Steve Carney. "A Building No Man Can Destroy." Morehead, Kentucky. September 16, 2001.

42

is still in our lives. He is still at work in our world. He is still with us…. He is present, 'Therefore we will not fear though the earth give way and the mountains fall into the heart of the sea. Though its waters roar and foam and the mountains quake with their surging…God is within her. She will not fall. Nations are in uproar, kingdoms fall, He lifts his voice, and the earth melts.' [He] is the one who is with us! When we are under attack, God is still with us. He is with you even in this place this morning." [62]

In the choruses, *"Surely the Presence"* and *"Holy* Ground," selected in a number of churches for the Sunday services following the September 11th tragedy, we hear an affirmation that God is always with His people. Consider the lyrics of both of these selections:

"Surely the presence of the Lord is in this place;
I can feel his mighty power and his grace;
I can hear the brush of angel's wings;
I see glory on each face;
Surely the presence of the Lord is in this place." [63]

"We are standing on holy ground;
And I know that there are angels all around;
Let us praise Jesus now.
We are standing in his presence on holy ground." [64]

When God's people can proclaim with confidence that God is with them, even in the midst of tragedy, the tragedy becomes bearable. We become confident that we can make it through the crises none the worse from the wear, even though we may have to navigate through a very difficult season of life.

---

[62] Carl Addison. "When We Are Attacked." Sikeston, Missouri. September 16, 2001.
[63] "Surely The Presence of the Lord Is In This Place" (Lanny Wolfe) ©1977 Lanny Wolfe Music/ASCAP/ rights controlled by Gaither Copyright Mngt. Used by Permission.
[64] "Holy Ground" Geron Davis © Meadowgreen Music/Songchannel Music (Admin. by EMI Christian Music Publishing) All Rights Reserved. Used By Permission.

Lesson 12: Profess God's Power

A second reason that Psalm 46 seemed so appealing to people immediately following the strikes on the World Trade Center and the Pentagon, was that these ancient words of life from this Psalm were able to give voice to the size and scope of the tragedy of September 11th; A tragedy, which for many felt as disconcerting and as a frightening as the major geological calamity described in that same text. Jim Lyon from the North Anderson Church of God in Anderson, Indiana, described the tragedy of September 11th in this way:

"What are we going to do? How can we make sense out of this, a time when the world seems to have been shaken, the foundations that we so often took for granted, the sanctity of American soil, [our] safety from foreign attack on this land, we call home…all that has been shaken. Just like [in] an earthquake, the ground that we have taken for granted, suddenly shifted. Now we're not sure if it will shift again, and that's very frightening."[65]

Many people across this nation were deeply impacted, even traumatized, by the strikes on the World Trade Center and the Pentagon. Not only were people horrified by the lives lost on the morning of September 11th, but also the sense of security that many felt prior to the events of the day collapsed as quickly as the Twin Towers. Because of the enormity of the devastation and loss of life, many people turned to Psalm 46 and, no doubt, found some comfort in the portrayal of the power of the sovereign God before whose voice the earth melted, and instruments of war were broken and burned.

A number of ministers across the country encouraged their people by reminding them that the all powerful God had not been caught off guard, but was, despite all appearances, still in charge and still on the throne.

Jim Lyon shared the following with his congregation the Sunday after the terrorist strikes:

---

[65] Jim Lyon. "Bad Spirit Removed". Anderson, Indiana. September 16, 2001.

"These awful days have disoriented us...How to respond? In these days, there are some important things for you to remember. First of all, God is still on the throne. Never forget that. We live in an age that is [part of] a cycle of history, and this cycle has been repeated many times. God, however, in that cycle always prevails, and though hell will reach up and seek to do mischief, God will prevail. He is still on the throne. The laws God established for the governance of the universe, the principal laws of the universe, are still operative. And no matter what happens, you know that the sun will come up, and that the rain will fall on the just and the unjust. [You know] the world has a sense of order about it, even when it seems to be chaotic. Know this also, that the moral order of the universe still stands. When people lash out at heaven, heaven will respond. When people do desperate things and criminal acts, there is a moral response. But in time, though the battle may be long, in time, we will seek and find justice. Make no mistake about it. God is still on the throne. Furthermore, not only is God on the throne, but Jesus is [also] Lord. You see, the God that we worship is not a God simply viewed through the lens of an Old Testament frame. Ours is a God who is most completely disclosed to us in the person, and in the work, of Jesus Christ the Lord. God is on the throne, and that [truth] is represented to us through His Son. The Word of God on the throne became flesh here on earth. Jesus is Lord. He is the Lord of Lords, the King of Kings; He is the master of all and He is ascended to be at the right hand of the Father. He is surveying the earth, and He is working in this world. The Living Christ still has a stake in what happens here. He is coming back. When He does, all things will be made right."[66]

Raymond Chin, from Chicago, Illinois, also reminded his congregation that God was still in charge. He made the following comments in his September 16th message:

"Put your trust in the Lord, because this event has proven to us that only God can protect us. We need to understand that freedom has a price. Freedom makes us vulnerable. Democracy makes us vulnerable.

---

[66] Ibid.

Because we are a democratic society, because we are a free society, there is some vulnerability with which we have to learn to live. And nobody can protect us from that, only God. Only God can provide that rock. So, David said, 'God You take me to a place that I can't go myself. You take me to that rock that is bigger than me, bigger than everybody else, and You put me on top of it, because only You can do it.' We take for granted the little inscription on our coin. 'In God We Trust.' We talk about it only when we run into a crisis. But the fact is, David says when your heart is overwhelmed we need to be led by God to a higher place where we can rest in Him, knowing that God is a refuge and strength, that He is a very pleasant help in trouble. Even though the world should change, and the mountains be lifted into the midst of the sea, God is still in charge. David said, 'God You lead me to the rock that is higher than me, because I am in trouble and my heart is overwhelmed...I can't protect myself, only You can protect me. So lead me to a rock that is bigger than me.'" [67]

The profession of God's power not only appears in the preaching following the September 11th strikes, but also was a major theme of the musical selections in the weeks immediately following.

A number of music selections for the Sunday, September 16th services following the terrorist strikes, illustrate the felt need to profess God's power in the face of this tragedy.

The worship leader, Linda Pinter, from the Scott Memorial Church in Chattanooga, Tennessee, made these remarks prior to doing a medley of songs, which included the popular worship chorus, *He Is Able*:

"This morning as I was reading in my devotion time, preparing my heart to be here to lead in worship, this is the Scripture that God led me to. And I wanted to share that with you because so many times as we don't trust in the Lord, as we don't seek His face, then things happen. And I want us, this morning, to realize that God is able. Last week, as the choir was in their retreat and we were standing around the campfire, about 11:00 P.M., the next medley of songs just started

---

[67] Raymond Chin. Chicago, Illinois. September 16, 2001.

46

flowing from all of us. And I was reminded again this week, 'that God is able, more than able, to accomplish what concerns me today.' He can handle anything that comes my way. And He can do more than I ever dreamed possible if I give Him permission."[68]

A number of surveyed churches sang this same worship chorus in their Sunday, September 16th worship services. Consider the lyrics of this chorus celebrating the power of God:
"He is able; more than able. To accomplish what concerns me today."

Another chorus chosen by a number of churches for the September 16th Sunday services was, *"Our God is An Awesome God."* The words give testimony to the sovereignty of God:
"Our God is an awesome God.
He reigns from heaven above with wisdom, power and love.
Our God is an awesome God." [69]

The popular worship chorus *"Shout to the Lord"* was chosen by several worship leaders to be sung in Sunday services across the country. A look at the lyrics reveals the work of a mighty God:
"Shout to the Lord all the earth let us sing.
Power and majesty praise to the King.
Mountains bow down and the seas will roar
at the sound of Your name.
I sing for joy at the work of Your hands.
Forever I'll love you; forever I stand.
Nothing compares to the promise I have in you."[70]

---

[68] Linda Pinter. "Is God Big Enough....To Bless Me." Chattanooga, Tennessee. September 16, 2001. "He Is Able" Rory Noland and Greg Ferguson © 1989 Maranatha Praise Inc. (Admin. by The Copyright Company, Nashville, Tennessee) All Rights Reserved. Used By Permission.

[69] "Awesome God" Rich Mullins © 1988 BMG Songs, Inc. (ASCAP) All Rights Reserved. Used By Permission.

[70] "Shout To The Lord" Darlene Zschech © 1993 Darlene Zschech/ Hillsong Publishing (admin the US and Canada by Integrity's Hosanna! Music)/ ASCAP

Some of the churches surveyed for this book chose more traditional hymns to give voice to the conviction that the God who sits on the throne is sovereign and mighty. Consider the lyrics of just a few of these selections:

A Mighty Fortress is our God

> ### *Verse 1*
> *A mighty fortress is our God, a bulwark never failing;*
> *Our helper He amid the flood of mortal ills prevailing.*
>
> *For Still our ancient foe Doth seek to work us woe—His craft and power are great, And armed with cruel hate, on earth is not his equal.*
>
> ### *Verse 2*
> *Did we in our strength confide, our striving would be losing?*
>
> *Were not the right man on our side, the man of God's own choosing.*
>
> *Dost ask who that may be? Christ Jesus it is He—Lord Sabbath His is Name*
>
> *From age to age the same, And He must win the battle.*
>
> ### *Verse 3*
> *And though this world, with evil filled, should threaten to undo us,*
>
> *We will not fear, for God has willed His truth to triumph through us.*
>
> *The prince of darkness grim, We tremble not for him—His rage we can en-*
>
> *dure, For lo, his doom is sure: One little word shall fell him.*
>
> ### *Verse 4*
> *That word above all earthly powers, no thanks to them abideth,*
>
> *The Spirit and the gifts are ours through Him who with us sideth.*

Let good and kindred go, This mortal life also-The body they may kill; God's truth abideth still: His kingdom is forever.[71]

Oh God, Our Help in Ages Past
Verse 1
O God our help in ages past, Our hope for years to come, Our shelter from the stormy blast, And our eternal home!
Verse 2
Under the shadow of Thy throne Still may we dwell secure; Sufficient is Thine arm alone, And our defense is sure.
Verse 3
Before the hills in order stood, Or earth received her frame, From everlasting Thou art God, To endless years the same.
Verse 4
A Thousand ages in Thy sight Are like an evening gone, Short as the watch that ends the night, Before the rising sun.
Verse 5
O God, our ages past, Our hope for years to come, Be thou our guide while life shall last, And our eternal home![72]

This is my Father's World
Verse 1
This is my Father's world, and to my listening ears All nature sings, and 'round me rings the music of the spheres. This is my Father's world: I rest me in the thought of rocks and trees and skies and seas- His hand the wonders wrought.
Verse 2
This is my Father's world, the birds their carols raise, the morning light the light the lily white, Declare their Maker's praise. This is my Father's world; He shines in all that's fair; in the rustling grass I hear him pass, He speaks to me everywhere.
Verse 3
This is my Father's world; O let me ne'er forget that though the wrong seems oft so strong, God is the ruler yet. This is my Father's

---

[71] Lyrics by Martin Luther.
[72] Lyrics by Issac Watts and music by William Croft.

49

world: Why Should my heart be sad? The Lord is king let heavens ring. God reigns let the earth be glad. [73]

To sense the presence of an all-powerful God in tragic moments helps to give us the confidence that we can indeed endure whatever crises we find ourselves facing. Anyone who has ever faced a personal tragedy will testify to the fact that tragedy has a way of sucking the very life right out of our bodies, and leaving us in a state of despair. In order to experience the peace of God during these awful times, we must proclaim God's presence with us in whatever state we find ourselves. Even as we profess His power available to us in the face of tragedy.

Chapter Two Questions For Discussion

1. If possible, review a recording of your worship service conducted September 16th. Did you sing a chorus or hymn in that service which may have emphasized either God's presence or power or perhaps both?

2. How might understanding God's presence in our lives help steady us in tragedy?

3. Why do you think songs about the power and presence of God were chosen by worship leaders to be sung immediately following the September 11th terrorist strikes?

4. Discuss a time in your life when you felt the Lord was particularly close to you.

5. How does the Lord make his presence known to us during our most difficult moments?

6. What insight did you gain about either the presence or power of God from reading this chapter? Explain.

7. How does God's power show itself in the lives of individuals?

---

[73] Lyrics by Maltbie D. Babcock.

Chapter Three
A Time To Mourn

"We see the sin of our people and our society and ask Your forgiveness. Jesus we bring to You right now our hearts that are so heavy and so full of sorrow and grief for the loss that has been sustained this week in these United States...God, Your heart as well is stricken with grief over the evil and over the horror of this week's events."

Mitchell Burch
Vancouver First Church of God
Vancouver, Washington

"We have experienced a national tragedy. Every one of us at sometime in our lives will also experience personal tragedies...People do wrong, and sometimes people suffer innocently. But, be assured God is also grieving over the events of this week."

Wayne Putman
First Church of God
Dallas, Texas

"We are here in the middle hour of our grief. So many have suffered so great a loss, and today we express our nation's sorrow. We come before God to pray for the missing and the dead, and for those who loved them. Now comes the names; the list of casualties is only beginning. We will read all of these names. We will linger over them and learn their stories, and Americans will weep. To the children, parents, spouses, families, and friends of the lost, we offer the deepest sympathy of the nation. And I assure you; you are not alone."

President George W. Bush
Friday, September 14, 2001

51

"Before you this morning is a very stark simple display, black satin surrounding a candle and fresh cut flowers. The black satin, of course, represents the tragedy, the horrific events that have taken place in our sister nation to the south. The candle represents the light that can only be shown in the darkness by God through His Son Jesus Christ and the church of Jesus Christ...The flowers represent the lives that were cut off, taken by the tragedy. There are very few words that can be said that could explain, describe or give expression to how we feel."

Dr. David Goa
Camrose Church of God
Alberta, Canada

"To grieve is to honor what God deems precious."

Jody Engel
Women of the Church of God

Macro Tragedy

September 11, 2001, may have been the darkest day in America's history. A shocked, horrified, and frightened nation watched as rescue crews raced toward the World Trade Center in New York shortly after American Airlines Flight 11 smashed into Tower One, creating a fireball of death and destruction. Flight 11 had departed from Boston that Tuesday about fifteen minutes earlier, bound for Los Angeles, California, and crashed without warning into Tower One at about 8:45 A.M. Eastern Standard Time. Then, at about 9:03 A.M., an already-shocked nation, many watching on television witnessed the crash of United Airlines Flight 175 into Tower Two. Approximately thirty-seven minutes later, American Airlines Flight 77 crashed into the west side of the Pentagon. By this time, the nation came to grips with the fact that a sinister and well-developed plot to murder and terrorize the citizens of the United States of America was being carried out across the nation. At 9:50 A.M., Tower Two of the World Trade Center crumbled to the ground in a deafening rumble, burying hundreds of

52

unsuspecting people under mountains of debris including many firemen, police officers, and emergency personnel who had been attempting to rescue office workers trapped inside. About forty minutes after Tower Two collapsed, sending dust and debris across lower Manhattan, Tower One toppled to the ground. At about 10:37 a.m. United Airlines Flight 93 crashed near Shanksville, Pennsylvania, after a group of brave passengers overpowered their hijackers and foiled a possible strike against the White House.[74] By mid-morning, on that dreadful day, four airliners had been hijacked, the Twin Towers of the World Trade Center lay in smoldering ruins, and the Pentagon was on fire in the nation's capitol. More tragically, 3,056 were dead. [75]

It is possible to get a sense of the enormity of this "macro" or national tragedy by reviewing comments made by ministers around the country given in their September 16th weekend services.

Dan Pinter, from Chattanooga, Tennessee, shared the following comments with his congregation on the Sunday after the terrorist strikes on the unsuspecting nation:

"Now, this has been some week hasn't it? If you are like me, I feel I am emotionally spent. If you think back about it folks, we have all been witnesses to the greatest act of mass murder in the history of our nation. The number of casualties is yet to be known. And here we are as a nation on the brink of possibly going to war with an enemy, as of yet not completely identified. It has impacted us all in a lot of ways. We had the state ministers' meeting this week; the two men we had scheduled to speak could not even get to the meeting because they were from out of state and could not fly in as scheduled. So, there was a lot of scrambling that had to be done to try to complete a program at the last minute. But, it didn't happen because the entire subject of conversation was what was on everybody's mind and what is going to happen? What next?"[76]

Following the terrorist strikes of September 11th, Randall Spence of Springfield, Ohio, shared with his congregation a message on the

---

[74] The Cincinnati Enquirer, 12 September, 2001.

[75] The USA Today, 30 May, 2002.

[76] Dan Pinter. "Is God Big Enough….To Bless Me?" September 16, 2001.

tragedy of Naomi, a woman who had lost her husband and both sons while living in Moab, from the Old Testament Book of Ruth. He had this to say as he described this bereaved woman's experience in that foreign land to members of his congregation who may have been feeling that same sense of loss after our nation's brush with terror:

"'For the Almighty has made life very bitter for me. I went away full, but the Lord has brought me home empty.' Perhaps Naomi's story is the story of many a person today. Perhaps this is the story of some of us, especially for people in New York and adjacent areas, '[we] went away full, but the Lord has brought me home empty.' I am sure that many persons within our nation feel this in light of the recent tragedy. The hijackings of the airplanes, the subsequent death of thousands of people, and all the innocent victims, both those on the airplanes and the families left behind; today you and I are stunned. We are sick and we are angered."[77]

Stephen Weldon of Andover, Kansas, was in Israel when the terrorist strikes against the United States occurred. Upon his return, he described his own sense of grief after hearing of the horrible news:

"We were just leaving the old city of Jerusalem, exiting out of the Joppa gate. Upon arriving at our bus, our bus driver, who spoke very, very little English, in Hebrew informed our guide, who then informed us, that a plane had hit the World Trade Center buildings. Needless to say, we were baffled by this news. In denial, we were thinking perhaps it was just a small Cessna, and things would not be so tragic. But, he went on to tell us that the buildings were gone. I couldn't even imagine such a thing, and hoped that surely his information was wrong. It made me physically sick to my stomach. My spirit was grieving and in pain. Immediately I wanted to come home to comfort and instruct our daughters, to really offer leadership at home. Though not feeling like doing anything, we went from there to the Shrine of the Book, the museum that houses the Dead Sea Scrolls, one of the greatest and important biblical archeological finds of all times. Confused and wondering what was happening back home, we went through the

---

[77] Randall Spence. "Why." Springfield, Ohio. September 23, 2001.

54

museum, while one man from our group, who was from New York and had friends in the World Trade Center buildings, tried to phone home. Upon leaving the museum, our bus driver informed us that the Pentagon had been hit, and that something had happened somewhere near Pittsburgh. We went deeper into shock. Outside the museum, we gathered in a large circle; I was asked to lead us in prayer. We then went back to the hotel and watched the horrifying and sickening live updates on CNN. We saw them along with you. We were in Israel, but our hearts were back home. We felt deep grief for the events, and we also felt the added pain of being in a foreign land wondering when we could come home. Now I know, we each have our own stories of these sickening events. We each could tell you where we were and what was going on in our hearts and minds, thoughts and feelings that have not gone away, thoughts and feelings that are not far from any of us, thoughts and feelings that linger much to out dismay. We know that they will not go quickly away." [78]

Carl Addison from his pulpit in Sikeston, Missouri, links September 11, 2001, with other earth shaking dates in American history. He offered the following comments in his September 16th message:

"December 7, 1941 - You already have an image in your mind, right? Nothing else had to be said but the date, even if you weren't around in 1941. When you hear somebody say December 7, 1941, already you know that [that day] was the day on which the Japanese attacked the United States at Pearl Harbor. History finds that date as a marker. November 22, 1963. Some of you remember that day like it was a week ago. And, some of you were nowhere near being alive yet. When you hear the date, if you were indeed around, you remember exactly where you were and what you were doing when you heard the news that the President had been shot in Dallas, Texas. It is a date that lives in our history, in our culture ingrained into us. And, even if you weren't around then, you know November 22, 1963, was a day that changed us as a nation. And, now there is September 11, 2001. Generations from now, people will look at that date just like they do

---

[78] Stephen Weldon. "Strong Tower." Andover, Kansas. September, 23, 2001.

December 7, 1941, and November 22, 1963. This date will be one of those markers in our history. The fact of the matter is everything changed with that attack. There were thousands and thousands of people who got out of bed, as was their routine in New York City and in Washington, D.C. They made their way off to work on a beautiful September morning, absolutely unaware that there were attacks being planned. And, everything changed with those attacks. We thought we were safe from the events that took place on our soil Tuesday. We thought those events were supposed to take place on foreign soil and in distant lands. We watch other people; nameless, faceless, people who live far, far away from us go through that stuff. In that moment, we became aware, like everyone else in the world, that we are vulnerable." [79]

In his Sunday, September 16th, message from Lexington, Kentucky, Stephen Birch simply shared the following stark truth: "Suddenly, there are no safe harbors. The physical and financial recovery from the terrible attacks of Tuesday is underway. But, the spiritual and emotional scars will take a long time to heal."[80]

Raymond Chin from Chicago, Illinois, attempted to give some perspective to the September 11th attacks on the United States in his September 16th message:

"The events of September 11th will be recorded as some of the most traumatic, the most disturbing, and the most catastrophic and life-changing, events in the history of America to this date. These events have transformed not only the skyline of New York City, but they have assaulted and wounded the American psyche more than we could ever explain. All of us watched in horror and disbelief, events that normally occur in Africa, Europe, the Middle East, or in some other less-developed countries. We see those things happen over there. Now, we are seeing them unfurling before our eyes. And, they are taking place in the good old USA. It looked like a movie…in fact; some

---

[79] Carl Addison. "When We Are Attacked." Sikeston, Missouri. September 16, 2001.
[80] Stephen Birch. Lexington Kentucky. September 16, 2001.

children still think it was a movie. Events we never thought we would see, events that we never thought would happen here, have shattered the façade of our invincibility, our power and might, our sense of safety and freedom." [81]

Personal Tragedies

I entered full-time ministry only days before the bombing of the Alfred P. Murrow Federal Building in Oklahoma City. I thought that, after the bombing which occurred on April 19, 1995, it might be worthwhile to produce for the Church of God movement a study of how the church responded to this tragedy during this watershed moment in our nation's history. For a number of reasons, that project was never taken up. Unfortunately, the events of September 11th gave rise to the need to think about and reflect on another national tragedy on a much more devastating scale. One of the reasons for writing this book was to aid us in reflecting on the messages and prayers lifted during those difficult days following September 11th. I am convinced that what was shared during those dark days can be applied to the personal tragedies that visit our lives from time to time.

As I busily shaped the beginning chapter of this book, examining the lessons we might learn by reflecting on American's worst national tragedy, I considered how frequently ministers have to help the members of their respective churches work through personal tragedy. The same week that I was completing the first draft of chapter one of this book, even as I attempted to process the national tragedy of September 11th, I was forced to deal with the personal tragedies visiting the lives of my people. On a Thursday afternoon, in the pastor's study, I listened to a saintly sister describe a serious medical condition that had nearly taken her life. On that afternoon, I made a call to the widow of one of my recently deceased comrades in ministry. This charming sister had lost her husband a few weeks earlier. She was feeling so alone, and to use her somber words, "barely making it." That Friday when I awoke, I received a message informing

---

[81] Raymond Chin. Chicago, Illinois. September 16, 2001.

me that one of the dearest members of our congregation had lost her daughter at a pitifully young age. All this happened on the heels of the deaths of both this dear saint's sister, and brother. That same morning, another call was received; on this occasion a fretting father worried aloud over his wayward son, "what should I try next to bring him back into line." After listening to each tragic dilemma, I am certain that not one of these calamities felt any less earth shaking and traumatic than the national tragedy of September 11th.

As I thought about the events of September 11th, the magnitude of this calamity and the lives affected by the reprehensible acts of violence carried out against innocent victims, I initially labeled this national tragedy a "macro" tragedy. I was, of course, juxtaposing this national tragedy against the "micro" tragedies or personal tragedies that occasionally visit the lives of all people. An example of a "micro" tragedy might be the loss of a family member, losing a spouse to divorce, a bout of depression, etc. The more I thought about the use of the terms "macro" and "micro" tragedy, the less helpful these terms became. I came to the rather obvious conclusion that there is simply no such thing as a "micro tragedy." I liken my use of the term "micro tragedy" to the way we use the term "minor surgery." The surgery can only be minor if the knife is used on someone else. We do not have the objectivity as feeling humans to measure the magnitude of a tragedy by the amount of people affected by the event. The fact is, the closer that tragedy comes to us, the more painful it is for us, even if we as individuals, or as family units are the only one affected by it. For example, it is a tragedy if a tornado blows through a residential section of a city and kills fifteen people. It is a profound tragedy if one of those people happens to be your spouse, or your child. Though national, the tragedy of September 11th may not have personally touched every American who watched it on television. It still is possible, nonetheless, to gain insight from those who processed this national tragedy through the lens of God's Word; insight that might be employed when we find ourselves facing tragedy in our lives.

58

Lesson 13: Following A Tragedy,
It Is Important To Take Time To Mourn And Grieve

A Time To Mourn

Ecclesiastes 3:4 tells us that there is a time to mourn or grieve. In other words, there is a season in our lives when the appropriate thing to do is simply to grieve and give voice to the profound pain of a broken heart. When we mourn, we are expressing the pain of separation from one that we love. It might be easy to pat the back of a friend or family member who has lost a loved one and say something like, "time will heal the wound." Those words, however, do little to honor the life of the person who has passed. On the contrary, they seem instead to elevate to the level of virtue one's ability to forget the loss of a loved one. We must be careful to remember that grieving is an act of love toward the deceased. We grieve and mourn because we have lost someone very valuable to us.

After the death of my first born son, Jacob Ryan Agee, to a rare heart defect, I wanted to move past the grief and to get back into my normal and familiar routine of life. I wanted to go to work, to run, to get back on a reading schedule. I wanted to live as if this tragedy had never occurred. At the time, I didn't realize how unfair this was to my deceased son "little Jake," who deserved a season of reflection and mourning, a season in which a father would mourn a broken relationship that this side of eternity would never blossom. What a horrible, devastating loss. Until my wife and I had our other five children, we didn't fully realize what we had lost when Jake was called to be with the Lord. Also, I did not recognize, at the time of Jake's death, my wife's own need to honor Jacob by mourning and grieving. Being Christians at the time, my wife Lori and I spoke about Jake being in a better place. For me, that almost gave me the excuse not to grieve over him. I should have known better. A curious and familiar story in the Christian Scriptures calls this kind of thinking into question. In John 11:1-46, Jesus had lost his friend, Lazarus, to death. He foreknew this tragic event, and also seemed to understand that this state would only be a temporary one, for He confidently affirmed the truth that Lazarus would rise from the grave someday. But, He also seemed to be suggesting that the plan was to raise Lazarus then and there. So, though Jesus knew that Lazarus would be raised immediately from the grave, and He knew that ultimately God would raise all His children in the resurrection at the last day, consider His behavior at the sight of Lazarus' tomb. He wept and apparently mourned and grieved so vigorously that the fellow mourners said, "Behold how He loved him!"

Jody Engel, in a letter sent to churches across America in November following the September terrorist strikes, discussed both the need to mourn and the nature of the grieving process:

"It is good to stop and linger in the sorrow, not to regroup our efforts to control, but to bend the knee to God and surrender to God's will. Solomon writes in Ecclesiastes 7:4, 'The heart of the wise is in the house of mourning.' James 4:9-10 exhorts us to grieve and to humble ourselves in the sight of the Lord, and He will lift us up. We grieve because it leads us back to God. We grieve because it leads us to worship. What does grief feel like? It does not feel like depression, which is sorrow unto death. Grief is sorrow unto life. There are various stages of grief, which do not necessarily follow an order. Denial comes and goes, anger may never fully leave, acceptance turns in hope for heavenly reunification. Grief is often avoided because it doesn't look very productive. When you are grieving, sometimes you sit quietly remembering; other times, you need someone to listen as you tell your stories. There are heavy days to acknowledge what will never be. Grief is reality of the here and hope for the not yet…. To grieve is to honor what God deems precious."[82]

Mourning For A Nation

If the citizens of this nation ever had a moment in their collective lives where it might have been appropriate to mourn and grieve, that

---

[82] Jody Engel. "Women of the Church of God publication." November, 8, 2001."

moment came on the morning of September 11, 2001. The horror of it all, unsuspecting employees beginning their workday, in New York and Washington D.C., trapped in burning buildings with no way of escape. Innocent civilians on jet liners on their way to work, or perhaps flying home, were unimaginably terrorized and then ruthlessly murdered. Americans all across the country watched in disbelief as people in desperation leaped from the World Trade Center towers to avoid being burned alive. We saw the loved ones of those who worked in the World Trade Center and the Pentagon going from hospital to hospital looking for relatives and coworkers with flyers in hand and tears streaming down their frantic faces. We listened to one heart-wrenching tale after another. There were, of course, the photographs of children in the arms of a missing father or mother as, the desperate spouse left behind described how much the departed one would be missed. Indeed, on September 11, 2001, and in the days and weeks that followed, it was appropriate for the citizens of this proud nation to mourn.

Mourning For A World

It is important to note that many ministers around the country wanted their people to know that despite the enormity of the tragedy of September 11th, God, as a matter of course, has plenty of opportunities to grieve. For this world can be an inhospitable place when people choose to live in rebellion to the commands of God's Word; His Word was given to ensure that we treat one another in loving ways. God never has a moment of vacation. He is painfully aware of the injustices, the violence and the greed that fills this world with grief and tears. Each tragedy that occurs under God's watch pricks his heart. Consider the following comments made by Steven Weldon of Andover, Kansas:

"What did God see on that day when these vicious and inhumane attacks took place? And, believers in Jesus… What should we see? In my limited understanding and thinking, it seems to me that in those few painful minutes as we witnessed these horrific events, you and I were given a glimpse in a way and in a form in which we could understand, [we were] seeing what God sees every day. As we saw thousands of lives being senselessly and needlessly sent into eternity as the results of the decisions of sinful men, we saw in a compacted space and time what God sees every day.... Friends, please understand the senseless and painful loss of thousands of lives is a sight that is before the eyes of our Heavenly Father every day. Because He is all knowing, and because He is ever present, the needless and painful destruction of tens of thousands of people as a result of the decisions of sinful men is before the eyes of our merciful, gracious, caring Heavenly Father. Every day on a global scale, God sees those who starve to death because of the decisions and greed of sinful men and because of the deception of our adversary. Every day on a global scale, God sees all the wars and skirmishes across this planet, and every life that is needlessly taken. Every day on a global scale, God sees those who are murdered out of greed, envy, hatred, and personal vengeance. Christians, though we desire to turn our eyes away from the carnage and pretend this horrendous thing had never happened, as ambassadors of God, we must learn to open our eyes and our hearts to see the world as God sees the world, see the world as a place that is far from perfect, as a sinful planet in which many people suffer and die, as a place that our adversary has greatly deceived, where sins run rampant, as a place that is desperately in need of a Savior, as a place that is desperately in need of God, as a place that is desperately in need of peace and hope, as a place that desperately needs only what God has to give through the only Savior of the world - His only Son, the one and only Messiah, Jesus. Do you see the world with new eyes? We should. As Elisha prayed for his servant in Second Kings, chapter six, verse seventeen, we need to pray for each other and ourselves. In this verse, Elisha prays, 'Oh Lord, open his eyes so he may see.' Then, the Lord opened the servant's eyes and he looked and saw the hills full of horses and chariots of fire all around Elisha. Fellow believers, with God's help, we need to open our eyes and allow our hearts to be opened by the things that break the heart of God, and thus develop a new compassion for those who are in slavery to sin, developing a new desire to tell as many people as possible about the forgiveness and peace and joy and hope and perfect love that can only come through Jesus."[83]

Rod Stafford from Fairfax, Virginia, shared this allied truth with his congregation on the Sunday after the terror attacks on the United States of America:

"I remind you of some things, not for shock value and not to in any way lessen the absolute tragedy of this event... Fifteen thousand people die every day just because they do not have enough food to put in their stomachs. Thousands upon thousands of people are physically and sexually assaulted every day. Thousands upon thousands of people have their lives every day taken away, brutally taken away - the old, the young, the unborn. Millions of people live every day on the edge of existence, not sure where their next day's sustenance will come from. I was reminded this week that, every time the Yellow River overflows in China, 10,000 people die. And, I just remind us of this to say... we have been forced to see up close and personal the pain and the suffering, and the brokenness that the God of this universe sees every moment of every day. I have often said that is why we could never view this world exactly the way God views it. We couldn't stand it emotionally."[84]

We see from these two excerpts, that God, in fact, views the suffering around the world constantly. In the shadow of September 11th, we are reminded that the world is a place that regularly experiences the tragedies of life, some caused by the sin of others, some seem to have no discernable cause at all. Taking the time to mourn is simply acknowledging what is going on in the heart of God. It is our valuing what He values. It is us getting on His page. God loves people; He grieves over the pain and loss people feel. Following the April 19, 1995, bombing of the Alfred P. Morrow Federal Building, I had this overwhelming sense that God was just as puzzled and broken hearted as the families of the victims searching the skies for some kind of answer. I wrote the following:

---

[83] Stephen Weldon. "Strong Tower." Andover, Kansas. September 23, 2001.

[84] Rod Stafford. "Discovering God's Purpose For Your Life." Fairfax, Virginia. September 16, 2001.

"On April 19, a bomb exploded in front of the Federal Building in Oklahoma City and our country was stunned. A teary-eyed nation looked toward the skies amid cries of the children and wondered aloud—'Why God? Why?' This question is born out of the conviction that God rules in the heavens and that He is just and loving. What happened in Oklahoma was an evil and a hateful act that brought grief to all who witnessed it. Most Americans reason that God could have stopped this terrible event from happening. Because the tragedy occurred, many are left questioning God's loving nature or for that matter His very existence…we must understand, however, that God's seeming inaction does not mean He is not moved. I, for one, am convinced that a teary-eyed God looks down on the rubble of a bombed out building, his eyes on the victims, on the children, and wonders silently, 'why man? Why?'"

Curiously enough, the Scriptures suggest, in the book of Genesis, that the cries of the victims of the sinful city of Sodom are the reason that the Lord finally destroyed it. The story seems to imply that the people in the city were, by their sinful behavior, causing such chaos and pain that even God could not emotionally endure the shrill cries of the victims. [85]

The extent of the love one person has for another, will determine how much he or she will mourn the loss of their unfortunate beloved. It is obvious that mourning and grieving is what one does when he or she loses something, or someone very valuable to them. Jesus himself grieved because of the underutilized potential of His people. He mourned because of the coming destruction his countrymen would have to endure as a result of their rejection of the Good News Jesus came to preach.

The Scriptures record Jesus' approach to the city of Jerusalem on his final visit:

"And when He approached, He saw the city and wept over it, saying, 'If you had known this day even you, the things which make for peace! But now they have been hidden from your eyes. For the

---

[85] Genesis 18-19

days shall come upon you when your enemies will throw up a bank before you, and surround you, and hem you in on every side, and will level you to the ground and your children within you, and they will not leave in you one stone upon another, because you did not recognize the time of your visitation.'" [86]

Mourning And Dancing

In the book of the Psalms, we find that there are not just songs of happy praise, but also songs that express the free, unfettered expressions of the sorrow, pain, and despair of living in a yet-to-be redeemed world. In our worship services, we haven't quite come to terms with how this kind of upsetting literature fits into our present understanding of authentic worship. While doing research for this book, I spoke with a well-known priest from a prestigious church in the Washington, D.C., area. As I spoke about what themes I was planning to discuss in this book, the topic of conversation turned to music. I explained that a number of the churches I surveyed had chosen upbeat and joyous praise choruses as part of their September 16th service line-up. In our conversation, the priest explained that he felt it might have been premature to make the transition from songs that allow congregations to reflect and to mourn in favor of the more joyous selections. Indeed, we may have prematurely moved from mourning to rejoicing on that Sunday after the September 11th, terrorist strikes. One minister, with training in crises counseling and who served at Ground Zero immediately following the World Trade Center attacks, explained to me that many people in the churches across our movement really don't know how to mourn and grieve.

I once did a funeral for a family in my congregation. During the service, a young man in the family lost control of his emotions in a fit of rage. We were burying his grandmother that day, and this man's mother, seated in the first row, had been diagnosed with cancer. I suspect he knew that she would also go very soon. He couldn't take it. He screamed, cursed, and shoved people to the side, even knocking

---

[86] Luke 19:41-44

one family member to the floor, before he was finally subdued and escorted out. This was the truest and freest expression of grief I have ever experienced.

Like the young man, the Psalmist doesn't hold back his grief. The Psalmist is, in fact, very open and genuine in describing the pain that he seems to have been feeling as he penned many of the psalms.

In Psalm 31:9-13, the writer records the following heartfelt words of grief:

"Be gracious to me, Oh Lord, for I am in distress; My eye is wasted away from grief, and my soul and my body also. For my life is spent with sorrow, And, my years with sighing; My strength has failed because my inquiry, And my body has wasted away. Because of all of my adversaries, I have become a reproach, especially to my neighbors. And an object of dread to my acquaintances; Those who see me in the street flee from me. I am forgotten as a dead man, out of mind, I am like a broken vessel. For I have heard the slander of many. Terror is on every side; While they took counsel together against me, They schemed to take away my life."

Psalm 69:1-12a also expresses a profound sense of sorrow:

"Save me, O God, For the waters have threatened my life. I have sunk in deep mire, and there is no foothold; I have come into deep waters, and a flood overflows me. I am weary with my crying; my throat is parched; my eyes fail while I wait for my God. Those who hate me without a cause are more than the hairs of my head; Those who would destroy me are powerful, being wrongfully my enemies, What I did not steal, I then have to restore. O God, it is Thou who dost know my folly, And my wrongs are not hidden from Thee. May those who wait for Thee not be ashamed through me, O Lord God hosts; May those who seek Thee not be dishonored through me, O God of Israel, Because for they sake I have borne reproach; Dishonor has covered my face. I have become estranged from my brothers, And an alien to my mother's sons….When I wept in my soul with fasting, It became a reproach. When I made sackcloth my clothing, I became a byword to them. Those who sit in the gate talk about me."

66

I find it very interesting that the Psalmist, David, the one who danced before the Lord in moments of sheer joy as when the Ark of the Covenant was being transported down from the house of Obed Edom to the capital city of Jerusalem, is also the one that just as freely mourns and weeps.

Would the Psalmist, who so freely danced in his moments of ecstasy, also have at times sung or prayed something like the lyrics of a song by Christian artist Dallas Holm?

Hungry babies dying every day
Doesn't seem much help is on the way
And I just don't feel dancin'.
There's a war each time you turn around
Seems like peace will never quite be found
And I just don't feel like dancin'.

Sure, I've got Your joy in my soul
And I am glad that Your love has made me whole
And I just don't feel like dancin'.

There's a young man tired of his life
Thinking maybe he'll just leave tonight
And I just don't feel like dancin'.

Little children missing by the score
I don't think I can take no more
And I just don't feel like dancin'.

There's a young girl dying in her heart
Stopped a life that she helped to start
And I just don't feel like dancin'.[87]

---

[87] "Just Don't Feel Like Dancing" Dallas Holm © 1985 Holm Made Music (Admin. by Music Services) All Rights Reserved. SESAC Used By Permission.

To be honest, I am not sure if the greatest of all worship writers and producer of many of the Psalms would fit in some of our worship contexts today. Because in them, the reality of tragedy and pain seems to be regularly ignored. The Psalmist, on the other hand, would not only dance on his good days, but he also felt the liberty to cry out to God when he found himself facing a crises in his life.

So, one of the appealing things about these Psalms is that they communicate to the Lord the reality of how the singer is feeling. There is a beauty in the honesty of these words. The Psalmist does not pretend everything is okay but, instead, pours out his soul to the Lord. Following the events of September 11th, a number of our leaders from across the movement seemed to offer this advice, "Follow the example of the Psalmist; 'don't bottle up your sorrow and grief; pour it out before the Lord.'"

As I was thinking about the material in this section of the book, I thought about the euphoric moments of my spiritual life. I also thought about those dark and desperate days. During my prayer time, I often walk on a secluded country lane. Recently, I thought about what kind of record might have been produced if my prayers, spoken aloud on that gravel road, would have been taped. There would have been a record of prayers filled with heartfelt gratitude and thanksgiving taped on my better days. But, there also would have been prayers recorded amid tears with screams and cries for help. In short, the work produced from the tapes of my prayer walks on that gravel road would look a lot like the Psalms. The Psalms seem to communicate to us that it is okay to express our hearts to the Lord. No matter what we might be feeling at the moment, joy or grief, there is no need to hold anything back. We can let it all hang out with Him. The Psalms express well the reality that God's people must walk not only on the tops of mountains, but also through the "valley of the shadow of death."

In his message, Wayne Putman from Dallas, Texas, reminds his congregation that the way we begin to recover from tragedy is to release grief:

"The Bible talks about how we are to recover from a tragedy like the one we have gone through, and from the tragedies that we will experience in our lives. We can begin to recover from a tragedy by releasing the grief.

Tragedy always creates strong emotion in us. Let me ask you, did you feel any emotions this week? I did, and I am sure you did too. There was fear; there was anger; there was worry; maybe there has been some depression that has been mixed in your life, maybe some resentment. Some of us don't know how to handle feelings too well. And, if we don't deal with them, and if we don't release them up to God, the recovery process takes so much longer than God ever intended. So, let me give you some thoughts from the Scriptures today that will help us release our grief to the Lord. You know many people, especially men, stuff down their feelings. We deny them; we ignore them…

But, look at the Scripture in your notes from I Peter 5:7. This is out of the Amplified Version, which really takes the Greek language and tries to amplify what God is saying through the original language of Scripture. It says, 'Cast the whole of your care, releasing or unloading the weight of it, all your anxieties, all your worries, all your concerns, once and for all on Him, for He cares for you affectionately, and cares about you watchfully.' Isn't that beautiful? And, that is what God tells us to do. We can choose. We have the free will whether we are going to cast our anxieties upon the Lord, or whether we are going to hold on to them and we are going to cringe back in fear and worry and be concerned…. How do you cast your cares upon the Lord? I think it is fairly simple. We bring the things that are on our hearts, the feelings that we [are experiencing], to God in prayer. And, then we release them to [Him] in faith. And, we keep on doing that until our feelings catch up with our faith. You know there are many of us today who are feeling all kinds of things. I have always been told that feelings aren't right or wrong; they aren't necessarily good or bad; but what we do with those feelings matter. And, the Lord said, 'Unload them. Get rid of them.' Lay them on Him and let Him begin to minister His care, and His watchfulness in our lives. But, we have to choose to do that. And I trust that you will choose to do that. If you haven't already, really get honest before God. God can handle our feelings. God can handle our fears, our anger, our resentment, and our wanting revenge, or whatever else you are feeling in your life. But He can't do anything in our hearts unless we choose to release our feelings up to Him. So, get alone with Him soon, today, and believe what His Word says, and keep on doing it, day after day after day until your feelings catch up with your faith. It is okay to grieve. It is okay to distress and to be sorrowful. And, I appreciate so much our President who has allowed us to be sad and to grieve this terrible moment of our history this week, and yet he has also had a faith that he has turned to the Word of God and to prayer."[88]

Following the events of September 11th, a real push was made by some ministers to emphasize the importance of faith and family versus all of the other items that sometimes vie for our time and attention. In the next chapter, we will look at lessons and insights gained with this theme in mind. It is important as we move to a discussion of properly ordered priorities to remember that tragedy national or personal has a way of helping us to remember what really matters most.

Chapter Three Questions for Discussion

1.) What new insights did you gain from reading this chapter?

2.) Select your favorite portion of Scripture from the Psalms. What emotion does this passage express?

3.) Describe your own emotional response to the horrific events of September 11th.

4.) Were you able to release these emotions in a healthy way following the events of September 11th?

5.) List four or five people with whom you would feel comfortable in their coaching you through tragedy. Why would you choose these individuals?

---

[88] Wayne Putman. "Recovering From Life's Disasters." Dallas, Texas. September 16, 2001.

6.) During past seasons of personal grief, in what Biblical passages did you find comfort?

7.) Identify a deceased individual you know and love. How do you remember and honor them?

Chapter Four
Keeping The Main Thing, The Main Thing

"Turn your eyes upon Jesus, Look full in his wonderful face. And the things of earth will grow strangely dim In the light of his glory and grace."[89]

"I believe that tragedies like this one really do force us to look again at our values. They force us again to look at the pursuit of our lives, to ask difficult questions about where we are headed as individuals and where we are headed as a nation."

Gary Kendall
Indian Creek Community Church
Olathe, Kansas

"One thing that we see in America today is that our focus has shifted.... We are no longer focusing on the Dow Jones Industrial Average; we are no longer focusing on our economic condition.... I watched as Democrats and Republicans put their arms around one another and stood on the capital steps and sang "God Bless America."... I want us to have resolve in our hearts to stay removed from self centeredness, and I pray that we will not go back to normal, that we will not go back to where we were."

Frank Curtis
Towne Boulevard Church of God
Middletown, Ohio

"The last week and a half for me has been such a reality check...Some of you have maybe seen more devastating things in your lifetime but for me it has been a huge reality check. I have found myself driving around Olathe, coming into my office, and going home to my apartment, and looking at so many things that once seemed so familiar and safe, they [seemed like they] would last forever. As I was driving around in these familiar places I realized that these places,

---

[89] Music and lyrics by Helen H. Lemmel .

are all temporary homes. Even when I looked at my own body, I was reminded of the reality that [it also is a] temporary home. It caused me to think about the things that are eternal and to ask the question, 'What lasts beyond all of this temporary stuff? What goes beyond the place that I live, the place that I work, and the place that I call my hometown? What goes beyond the things that my eyes can see right now?' It was just such a reminder that God, the creator, and who I am, my inmost being, these things last, these things are eternal. The things that I see everyday with my eyes are temporary. What is crazy about this, is that we give so much time and energy and attention to things that are temporary. A lot of times we give less time and energy and attention to things that are eternal."

Jennifer Hunt
Indian Creek Community Church
Olathe, Kansas

Lesson 14: Be Diligent To Keep The Main Thing, The Main Thing

As a result of the examination of how the Church of God Reformation Movement ministers and leaders handled the attacks on September 11th, we learn how important it is to "keep the main thing, the main thing."

In his prophetic message delivered from Menlo Park, California the Sunday after the terrorist strikes on the United States, Paul Sheppard describes a nation whose priorities had strayed way off the mark. He explains how this nation had invited God out of its national life:

"Except the Lord build the house, except the Lord guard the nation, you are in trouble. And remember we invited Him out of our business as soon as we become prosperous. We said, 'we got it from here.' Thank You for helping us in the struggling days. But we got it from here. So, now we are spending our time in court, in the Supreme Court with cases trying to get, 'In God We Trust,' off the money, and the Ten Commandments off the walls of public buildings. We have decided that we don't need God in the consciousness of our nation. So

74

since we have invited Him out of our business; He cannot protect us; He cannot hover over us. And the result is we are not secure. We never were secure; we were just cocky."[90]

The tragic events of September 11th, if only temporarily, went a long way to remedy this corrupted sense of what is most important in life. This is very accurately described in the above comments.

Immediately following the terrorist strikes of September 11th, the concern of millions of people across this nation shifted dramatically from putting in another day at the factory, church or office, project deadlines, presentations, or trading stocks and bonds, to those desperate victims of this horrific and violent act. Some of those victims were seen on television trapped high above the ground in two real life towering infernos. Others were frantically searching for lost friends, family members and coworkers, while others lay injured from falling debris. On that terrible day, during this nation's hour in the crucible, the priorities of many of its citizens changed. Offices closed, schools let out early, and many athletic events around the country were cancelled. It was a truly astonishing to witness how the people of this nation reordered their priorities. Faith in God, love for family, and concern for fellow friends and coworkers, as well as a strong and vibrant patriotism, were reborn in the hearts of millions during this very bleak period in our nation's history.

Rod Stafford shared some of his insights on tragedy and priorities on September 16th from Fairfax, Virginia. In this message he related how this particular tragedy shaped his own set of priorities on that dark day in September. He begins by recalling a television interview in which the commentator was questioning some of the athletes about the decision to cancel the scheduled weekend games:

"They were interviewing some of the players about how they felt about that decision. I happened to have the TV on when [one particular player] was being interviewed. His response kind of captivated me, so

---

[90] Paul Sheppard. "An American Tragedy In Biblical Perspective." Menlo Park, California. September 16, 2001.

I went and wrote it down. I wanted to remember it. This is what he said when he was asked about that decision. He said, 'Well, I am glad they made that decision. Given what has happened, winning a football game just doesn't seem that important.' Now, of course, he is right. But here is the deal....It never was really that important. Now half of you are laughing, and the other half are saying, 'Watch it buddy! You are talking about sacred stuff here.' So ... Not only was it never that important, neither are so many of the things that we give so much of our lives to. There are so many things that we give so much of our lives to. Given what is going on, we say they're really not that important. But the reality is that they have never really been that important. They have crept their way up the priority list...Every so often because of some kind of event in the world, a whole community, a whole nation, has a little window open up. And through that window for a brief moment, they are able to see life as it really is. They are able, for a moment, to see what is really important in life. For a moment, they are really able to see what are the essentials of life, what they should focus their lives on. For a brief moment, regardless of where they are in their faith, whether they know Christ or not. Sometimes, events are so overwhelming that this window opens up and for a brief moment, everybody within that country, everyone within that nation, or that community peers through that window and they see life as it really is. Then, that window closes. And life, for many people, goes back to business as usual. I have heard several times this week, the statement, 'Our country has been changed forever by this event.' Have you heard that statement in some form or fashion? My response to that has been, 'No, we haven't been changed forever by this event.' Our freedom to move about, and to go where we want to go, when we want to go there, and the timing to go there may be limited for a little while. We may feel more patriotic for a while. The way we fight wars may profoundly change. But, we as people have not been changed forever. The window will close, and things that are really not that important will seem important again. For many, their priorities will go back to the same priorities they had before all this occurred. The window will close. Things that seemed silly to worry about, in light of everything that is going on, people will begin to worry about again. I can't tell you how many times this week I have heard that statement. 'Well, in light of everything that is going on, it seems petty to be worrying about that.' At 9:05 A.M., on September 11th, at almost the exact moment that the second plane was flying into the World Trade Center, I was in the auditorium of Fairfax County Government Center for the hearing with the board of zoning appeals about the rezoning of our property over on Braddock Road, something that we have been asking you as a congregation to be praying about. I was there with other people from our congregation. We presented our case… Now, I came out of that meeting unaware of everything that had gone on. I got in my car. I have to confess to you, that even though I realized that the news wasn't really that bad, that it just really meant that three more weeks were going to have to go by… I was, in my spirit frustrated and worried… frustrated that it was going to take another three weeks, and that we were going to have to go through more detail, even though it was stuff we were going to have to do later down the line. I was just kind of bothered by all of that. I was fussing and fuming, and pulled up outside of our house, and went inside. As I walked in our front door, I saw my wife, Donna, sitting in our little foyer, really, almost in the fetal position, just kind of rocking back and forth, with kind of a horrified look on her face. She just pointed into our family room at the TV. I turned that corner and I looked at all of the things that had gone on in that hour that I was in the government center. We sat there together and watched the events unfold. We watched as the second tower of the World Trade Center collapsed into this smoldering heap. After a while… Donna turned to me and she said, 'Oh, by the way, how did your meeting go?' At that point, even though I was disappointed, still… I wasn't worried about it anymore; I wasn't feeling very frustrated about it anymore. I found it pretty easy to turn it over to the sovereignty of God and say, "God, I am going to be obedient to Your Word, I am not going to worry about this, I am just going to trust in You. You are in charge." I found it fairly easy to do that. Maybe you can relate to that [story] this week, maybe there has been this little window and it has been much easier to kind of say, 'Yeah, no need to worry about this. This is silly stuff to worry about; I just [need to] turn this over to the Lord.' But folks, let me tell you, that

77

window will close again for many people. Once again, they will start worrying about little silly things that God says, 'I don't want you worrying about that. I want you to trust Me on this.' The window is going to close, and people that are now willing to set aside petty differences, partisan rhetoric, because of a common enemy, will go back to engaging in small minded attacks on one another. The window will close and people who for a moment are willing to set aside selfish ambition and love their neighbor as they love themselves will go back to pursuing power and wealth, and looking out primarily for number one."[91]

One of the things that tragedy does for us is it helps us put everything into proper perspective. A close acquaintance of our family recently received some devastating news. Without radical surgery and a successful battery of treatments he was given only a year to live. With the treatment he was given only a twenty or thirty percent chance of survival. As I discussed with him what impact this shocking and horrific news had on him, he pointed out a change in the way he prioritized his life. First, he said, the most important thing was to have one's relationship with the Lord right. Secondly, he pointed to his granddaughter playing there at his knee and said, "She is what is important." In that discussion, he mentioned the importance of God, family, and love in general in one's manner of relating to others. These items topped his list as he walked in the shadow of a devastating personal tragedy. Though this gracious gentleman who had been out of church for many years acknowledged his ignorance of the Bible in that conversation, he really seemed to have the right ideas with regard to the way he had reprioritized his life following the news of his illness.

One of the lessons or insights learned from the September 11th terrorist strikes, is that tragedy has a way of highlighting what is really important in life.

Steve Chiles, from Phoenix, Arizona was stranded in Oklahoma City by the terrorist strikes of September 11th and was forced to

---

[91] Rod Stafford. "Discovering God's Purpose For Your Life." Fairfax, Virginia. September 16, 2001.

commute home by a rental car. He speaks here of the effect tragedy has on our list of priorities:

"Tragedy gives us a renewed sense of priority…. Isn't it amazing how in the wake of tragedy everything that is important suddenly becomes clear? Really interesting, you saw as you were watching the television, you saw the accounts of people who were making calls at the last moment from the top of the World Trade Center knowing they were not going to get down, calling their families to tell them one last time, 'I love you.' People calling from the back of airplanes, they knew they were not going to get out of to tell their families one more time, 'I love you'…All I wanted to do was to be at home and to be with my wife and be with my kids. Because suddenly, in the wake [of tragedy,] the things that are really important, man, just stand out! Amen?"[92]

Stephen Weldon from Andover, Kansas, offered the following comments on how this tragedy impacted the way in which we prioritize our lives:

"The events of September 11th, in just a very brief period of time, shook much of the world into realizing that many of the things in which they had trusted were no longer as valid or as stable as they thought. It forced them to reconsider and reevaluate what was really important. People around the world… have been forced to reevaluate, reexamine and reconsider the things in which they had trusted… When the towers of the World Trade Center collapsed, the things in which many people trusted also collapsed. In many ways, these huge monoliths symbolized power and security and wealth and freedom, the American way, a secure and sound economy in an untouchable country. Therefore, when these buildings were shattered, the trust and hope of many were also shattered. How about your hopes and dreams? How are they? In what do you trust? Are the things in which you trusted still standing? Friends, we have been overwhelmed by bad news, but in the midst of all of this tragedy I also have some wonderful and glorious news. Could you use a little wonderful and glorious news

---

[92] Steve Chiles. Phoenix, Arizona. September 16, 2001.

right about now? Please listen very carefully to this. Please know there is one tower that will never be shaken, there is one tower that evil can never shatter; there is one tower that evil men can never bring low and scatter its rubble in the streets; there is one tower that will ever stand for the freedom, power security, hope and a glorious future."[93]

Mark Richardson had this to say regarding how the tragedy affects our sense of what is really important:

" Tragedy helps us to return our attention in life to the things that really matter. So many people realize, some far too late, that what really matters in life often escapes our notice until it is threatened or taken away. The truth of the matter, is that I am sure that no one in those buildings or on those planes when all of that was happening and their lives were hanging in the balance, I am sure none of them wished that they could finish that day's work. I am sure none of them were concerned perhaps even getting a raise or going on another vacation or buying a new Lexus or fighting with a coworker. I am sure none of them were concerned about getting tickets to the Jets or the Giants game or the Redskins game on Sunday. I am sure they weren't concerned about any of that kind of stuff. But they began to think about their families. They began to think about their God. They began to think over the course of their lives to see if all of their striving in life was just chasing after the wind. You see, Jesus tells us in the Word that we can 'gain the whole world and lose our soul.' Now there was a play that was written that says you can't take it with you. Some have tried. Some have even had them put their wealth and possessions in their casket with them, only to find that there is no where to spend it in the grave. And no one in hell takes the kind of currency that you bring. We often need a reminder about what is really important in our lives. We often need a wakeup call that all of our striving and seeking after gain in this world is sinking sand, building a house without a foundation. We need to begin to make the main thing, the main thing.

[93] Stephen Weldon. "Strong Tower." Andover, Kansas. September 23, 2001.

We need to focus on what really matters in life. We need to boil our lives and activities down to the very essence of what matters in life."[94]

Marty Grubbs from Oklahoma City, Oklahoma, makes some comments on shifting priorities, and then described how the events of September 11th impacted the scheduled activities of that day's planned staff retreat:

"When we woke up Tuesday morning, there were, no doubt, a variety of things weighing on our minds, the routines of the day... commitments. We had the usual concerns, as well as the ongoing concerns we probably carry about our families, or our health, or our finances. But by 10:00 A.M. on Tuesday morning, most of what had passed through our minds to that point seemed so trivial. In some cases, completely meaningless. At the [moment of the tragedy], our lives changed probably for the rest of our lives. In some ways we will never be the same again as Americans. The pastoral staff had gone away a couple hours from here at one of our state parks for a retreat just to be together. We do this at least once a year to pull away to think, to pray, to be together, to seek God's will on how we should lead this congregation as pastors. We had a great Monday, and a great Monday evening. Our sessions together were rewarding and very special, but Tuesday morning when we came back together in the conference room, and we began to get just the bits and pieces of what was happening on that day, so quickly, it became clear that all the many concerns represented by the eighteen of us sitting around that table...were quickly whittled down to one basic thing, that is [the truth of] Jesus Christ the Hope of Glory. At that moment, that is what really mattered...Jesus Christ the author and perfector of our faith, Jesus Christ the hope of the world, Jesus Christ the sacrifice for our sins, Jesus Christ the giver of eternal life to those who will receive Him and believe in His name."[95]

Idolatry: The Sin Of Misplaced Priorities

---

[94] Mark Richardson. Pittsburg, Pennsylvania. September 16, 2001.
[95] Marty Grubbs. "Struck Down...But Not Destroyed." Oklahoma City, Oklahoma. September 16, 2001.

When we discuss idolatry, we often think of half clothed natives dancing around a large moss covered, stone representation of a god tucked in some distant and tropical jungle. It may be that the reason why idolatry is the first prohibition listed in the list of the Ten Commandments is simply because of the fact that we as humans are so prone to it. We seem to have a propensity within us to forget what is essential and most critical in life. The first two of the Ten Commandments serve as a corrective to this impulse.

God's people in the Old Testament were given a list of commandments that were to order their lives. These commandments were to serve as boundaries inside of which a blessed life could be lived. We find these commandments listed first in the book of Exodus. The first three commands deal with one's relationship to God, while the final seven have more to do with an individual relationship with other individuals. In other words, what seems to be most important to God is that He is the first item on our priority list. He wants to be in intimate relationship with us. It is impossible to read the Bible and not hear God calling to us, "I want to be your friend." He wants to be at the center of our lives. Dare I think it or say it? We make His life richer and fuller by choosing to be near Him. The command from the Old Testament even suggests a hint of a lover's jealousy toward His beloved:

"I am the Lord your God, who brought you out of the Land of Egypt, out of the house of slavery. You shall have no other god's before Me. You shall not make for yourself an idol, or any likeness of what is in heaven above or on the earth beneath or in the water under the earth. You shall not worship them or serve them; for I, the Lord your God am a jealous God, visiting the iniquity of the fathers on the children, on the third and the fourth generations of those who hate Me."[96]

In the Sermon on the Mount given by Jesus in Matthew 6:33, Jesus tells His followers to, "Seek first His kingdom and His righteousness."

---

[96] Exodus 20:1-5.

In other words, He was saying, "Place God, His agenda, and His work first on your list of priorities."

In his message the week after the terrorist strikes of September 11th, Gary Kendall from Olathe, Kansas, discusses how the tragedy had shaped his own thinking about priorities:

"When I saw the plane crash into the World Trade Center I ran upstairs. I saw the second plane crash into the second tower. I was just sick. Then, within a few moments, I heard the report about the Pentagon, and saw pictures of the gaping hole in it. My head and heart raced to people that I love who were traveling…So many emotions came flooding into [my] mind and into [my] heart…Tragedy makes us realize what matters most. This does need to be a spiritual gut check in our individual lives and [in the life of this] nation… Many times we value political correctness in our country over righteousness…we [value] the pursuit of pleasure, of leisure, work or prosperity. We place these above righteousness, above godliness, above prayer, or service…Jesus talked about this in Matthew 6:32–33. He said, 'Your Heavenly Father already knows all of your needs.' He knows that you need to have a certain level of income. He knows you need rest. He is the Author of things that are pleasurable. But all of them have their right place, and that is underneath our devotion to Him. Jesus said, 'Your Heavenly Father knows you need these things. He will give you all you need from day to day.' He is promising us that. It isn't like we have to pursue it on our own, if we will live for Him and make the kingdom of God our primary concern. It is real simple; He says, 'put Me first.' Put God first in these days…. Remember what matters most, and put God first. There is a Scripture in the Old Testament when the prophets are going to the nation of Israel. Israel had turned from God and was pursuing its own way. As a result, difficult times were coming. The prophet said to the people, 'Return to God and He will return to you.' I think those words are most appropriate today to us as individuals." [97]

---

[97] Gary Kendall. "What Matters Most." Olathe, Kansas. September 16, 2001.

Lesson 15: Our First Priority Should Always Be God

Whether we find ourselves in the midst of a tragic situation or not, we should be able to confidently affirm that the Lord has the first place in our lives. God should have this privileged place; He should be given the best of our time, our resources; he should be honored above all, and given the directional control of our lives. It is important to recall that when we decided to become a follower of Jesus, we accepted a new CEO into our lives. No longer do we call the shots, but rather, the Lord is given the directional control. [98]

Jesus was communicating the importance of having God at the top of our lists of priorities when He answered the question of a lawyer who was seeking to discover the most important of all commands. In this passage of Scripture Jesus gave the following answer in response:

"You shall love the Lord your God with all your heart, and with all you soul, and with all of your mind. This is the great commandment. The second is like it. 'You shall love your neighbor as yourself.'" [99]

**Lesson 16: Our "Second" First Priority
Should Be People**

Though the lawyer in the above mentioned passage, asked of Jesus only one command, the Lord did a wonderful thing instead; He gave him an attachment, or addendum. He said that not only should God be

---

[98] My, how we need a good dose of this teaching in the Reformation Movement today. Even the spiritual folks in our congregations who have ownership of the ministry need to revisit who is to be in charge. Jesus is the head of the church. The church has never been, nor should it ever be a democracy. Had the church in Jerusalem been asked to admit Saul in Acts 9, it would have never happened. God himself made that top-shelf decision. Had the church voted on whether or not to allow the Gentiles into its ranks, it wouldn't have happened. God told Peter to do it, over Peter's objections. The church has a Leader, a Shepherd. Not only does She have a chief shepherd, but She also has junior shepherds who have been given the task of overseeing the flock. With that office comes more authority than some might want to admit. Having said this, however, the task of the pastor-leader remains today to submit to the Lord first, and to lovingly call his or her flock to do the same.
[99] Matthew 22:37-39

on one's lists of priorities, but people should also be at the top of that list of priorities. There is profundity in the realization that the great command addresses not only the quality of one's relationship to God, but also the quality of one's relationship to other people as well. In fact, Jesus is suggesting that the two commands are inseparable. God and people belong together on the top of the rightly ordered list of priorities. If we place God in His rightful spot at the top of our respective priority lists, then we will naturally elevate people to the top of that list as well.

Lesson 17: God Wants Our Relationships
To Be Fuelled By Love

Not only is God stating that He and humanity should rightfully share the spot at the top of a rightly ordered priority list, but He is also stating that the quality of all relationships is critical. The fuel behind those rightfully ordered relationships should be love. I experienced a real eye opening realization some months ago. So many of the Fruits of the Spirit listed in the book of Galatians are, in fact, attributes and qualities which allow one individual to live in harmony and rich fellowship with another: love, patience, kindness, goodness, gentleness, and self control. The Fruits of the Spirit not listed in my above example seem to have a communal element: joy and peace. These last two fruits can't be experienced in isolation. I believe passionately that the abundant life Jesus came to offer can only be found in the cross hairs of a righted relationship with God and the people in one's relational network. Anyone that is married, or has a teenager, or a mother-in-law knows that this "ain't easy." [100]

Jesus gives us the Great Command and the Lord, in the Old Testament, gives us the Ten Commandments simply because He wants us to experience abundant life. We can live abundantly, fully, peacefully and richly only when we right our relationship with God and when we right our relationships with the people in our relational

---

[100] I am, of course excepting my own lovely and supportive wife, my charming mother-in-law, and my delightful teenage son.

network. If we read the Scriptures carefully, there is something even to be gained by righting our relationships with our enemies. I believe the Bible places such a premium on forgiveness simply because forgiveness allows strained and broken relationships to be mended. For us to experience the fullness of life, we have to love one another and the Lord. I find that many that come into my church and into the churches of my able colleagues want some quick fix of happiness, joy and peace. Many of these hurting people have serious relational issues that need to be addressed. Joy and peace can only be found when these relationships are righted. [101]

Lesson 18: God Has Called Us To Love All People

The events of September 11th were calculated and carried out by the Al Qaida network of Islamic extremists who have made the citizens of the United States their avowed enemies. One experiencing tragedy may find that a particular individual is the cause of their intense pain and brokenness as was the case of the families of the victims of September 11, 2001. In such cases, the survivors are forced to negotiate their way through not only tremendous grief but also intense, white-hot anger. Our Lord calls us to right our relationships with all people including our enemies. Only then can we live life to the fullest.[102]

Lesson 19: We Can't Love People Too Much

---

[101] I am a believer in the extraordinary power of God. I do, however, think that people who come to church are mistaken if they believe the church has a quick and easy remedy for the chronic pain they feel as a result of a broken or unhealthy relationship. These hurting souls may need more than a pop on the head or even a sincere prayer at the altar. I am inclined to agree with Dr. Billy Ball, longtime pastor of the Towne Boulevard Church in Middletown, Ohio who taught me that whether or not a person will be happy in this world, depends more on the quality of their marriage than on any other single factor.

[102] I believe the decision to love an enemy is the critical element in loving an enemy. God has oceans of love available for the one who choose to draw on His vast reserves.

86

One of the things that fascinates me about keeping a journal is tracking how I have matured in my thinking over time. I was married to my wife, Lori, in December of 1987. As I read through the entries in the months that lead up to our wedding date, I sense an anxiousness over loving my soon-to-be bride too much, and consequently drawing the displeasure of the Lord. In my mind, my love and my devotion for my wife-to-be, was in competition to my devotion to the Lord. The fact is, God was growing my love for my wife during the time leading up to our marriage. It was His desire that this special love multiply, mature and grow. The more I loved my wife, the more I was becoming like the Lord.

I am certainly aware of the fact that if I were forced to choose between pleasing God or pleasing a person dear to me, God must come first. Having said this, however, as I grew in my understanding of the Christian faith, I came to realize that it is impossible to love someone too much. On the contrary, one's ability to love God who the Scriptures reminds us cannot be seen, is enhanced and stretched by exercising one's love for people. When you love people you are doing the work of the Lord. When you love people a lot you are doing the work of the Lord better. I am going to go out on a limb and say, "You never have to worry that God will get His feelings hurt because you love a person too much." The fact is, when we love people deeply we are doing imperfectly what God does profusely, perfectly and without limits. [103]

Lesson 20: Every Day Is A Valuable Gift From God

When Stones Cry Out

---

[103] Again, the church is called to love those it serves. We will never reach this world until we fall in love with it. (Chances are not very good that the Lord will be back any time soon if we have to preach the gospel to the world first.) Because we preach the good news best when we love the ones we are called to reach. We can't even find it in our hearts to love the sexually deviant among us, let alone the Hindu in some distant, sun parched part of the world.)

A few years ago, I wanted to do some writing about perspectives gained from surveying stone markers, and their inscriptions, in some of the nineteenth century cemeteries found in the rural community of West Elkton, Ohio. One of the insights that I gained from this reflection is that every day we have on this earth is priceless and should be appreciated fully. If you read some of the inscriptions on these old, mossy stones, you see that one of the practices was to include the exact number of days a person lived. For example, the stone may read, "Henry Gifford, eighty-one years, ten months and four days." We no longer include the exact number of days a person lived on their gravestone. What was the reasoning behind this practice? Why did they do it? Could it have been their sensitivity to the fact that everyday is a precious gift that needs to be appreciated, and lived to its fullest?

This is also a lesson that the events of September 11th taught people across the nation. We are not promised tomorrow, or even the rest of this day. The fact is, that on the eleventh day of September 2001, many people went to work having no idea that they would not be coming home. Life looks so different in the shadow of death. We seem to appreciate it only as we see it nearing its end. We could live better if we remembered that when we wake up, regardless of the side we choose to rise from, we already are the recipients of the goodness of a gracious God.

Lesson 21: Every One Of Our Relationships Is Important

A second insight from the stone markers that I found to be very important has to do with our relationships. God's most profound way of enriching us is by placing people into our lives. As I walked among the stones reflecting on the venerable markers lining my community's cemetery, I noticed that not only are family members buried near one another, but oftentimes written on the stone marker is the relationship of one individual to another. For example, "Mary Ellen Stubbs, Our Mother." Or, "Elizabeth Ann, infant child of David and Ruth Ann Stubbs." These relationships were apparently important enough to those living many years ago to carve them in stone for posterity. Relationships rank high on God's priority for His people. I learned this not only from Scripture but also from a series of events during a painful period in my own life. Following a tumultuous year in my home church, many individuals left to form a new work. Obviously, this was a painful time for our family. Some of the relationships with individuals who decided to leave the church were strained to the limit before their departure. Not long after the split, one of the members of our congregation passed away. I had planned to arrive early at the viewing. A very curious set of circumstances delayed my arrival. During that period of delay, it dawned on me that perhaps I was being held up by the Lord for a purpose. Sure enough, when I did finally arrive and subsequently worked my way out of the funeral home, I met one of the couple's whose feelings for me were quite raw. We chatted a few moments. From that meeting I relearned the truth that God places a very high value on our relationships, even those relationships that aren't always comfortable.

Getting Our Relationship With God Right

If you feel that you haven't allowed God to be first in your life, He desires to be as close to you as you do to Him. Make the decision that you want to follow Him. Take the time now to pray the following prayer:

Heavenly Father,

Please forgive me for my past sins. I want be in right relationship with You. I want to restore You to Your rightful spot as the Lord of my life. Please come into my life now. I believe Jesus Christ died so I can be forgiven for my sins. I believe You raised Him from the dead. I acknowledge that You put a very high premium on the lives of the people around me. I give You my whole heart now. In Jesus' name.

In the next chapter, we will look at what can be learned from the tragedy of September 11th with regard to the "Why Question." In addition, we will take a deeper look at the role evil and free choice played in the events of September 11th particularly, and in an imperfect world generally.

Chapter Four Questions for Discussion

1.) A number of ministers declared that this nation had missed the mark with regards to its setting of priorities. Do you agree with this assessment? Explain.

2.) How does the sin of Idolatry demonstrate itself in popular American culture?

3.) What advice would you offer a friend or colleague who you believe might be making a poor financial decision that would result in years of financial stress?

4.) In this chapter I suggest that it is impossible to really love someone too much. Do you agree? Explain.

5.) How has misplaced priorities in the lives of God's people diminished the effectiveness of the church?

6.) Identify an individual in your church who you think has a well- ordered list of priorities. Why did you choose this person?

7.) What strategies have you found effective in "keeping the main thing the main thing?"

Chapter Five
The "Why" Question

"I think the most popular question...everyone is wanting to ask is, why? Why did this take place? Why would anyone do such a thing, knock down two buildings, damage the Pentagon, crash several planes and take so many innocent lives?.... Our God is everywhere; He knows everything. Only He understands why... innocent people have to suffer. I truly believe that our minds and our intellect are nowhere near the level and capacity of God's. Therefore, we cannot understand, even if we tried, why things happen as they do."

Paul Mumaw
First Church of God
St. Joseph, Michigan

"The rescue workers, the volunteers, those who lined up to give blood and to give money, all remind us today that evil does not triumph. Wickedness does not win. There is still good and beauty in our world, even in a week as ugly as the one we have just been through."

Dr. Timothy Clarke
First Church of God
Columbus, Ohio

"America...must hunt down the terrorists. They are evil. The men who planned and ...slaughtered thousands of innocent people are evil. The world is not safe when evil is in control. The world is looking to America to control the forces of evil. In World War II it was Nazism. Then during the cold war it was Communism. The events of the past week remind us that evil does exist, that there is a devil. There is a right way and a wrong way; there is good and bad. Listen, the world is not safe when evil is in control. Evil must be conquered. If that is true in the nation...let me remind you...it is true in our lives. You must not let evil control you. If you let evil control you, it will destroy you."

Dr. Daniel Harden
Kendall Church of God
Miami, Florida

"The lethal attack upon the World Trade Center and the Pentagon, and the crashing of American airliners, has shocked the sensibilities of freedom loving people around the world. Though the perpetrators of this violence have yet to be fully identified, there is no mistake of what was behind this assault upon our nation - Evil."

Ron Fowler
Arlington Church of God
Akron, Ohio

"Last Tuesday morning, our country and our world was shocked by the attack of terrorists against our nation. [This attack] resulted in massive loss of life and property. It was an inhumane act done by individuals, whom it would seem, were devoid of any shred of human kindness. They are perfect examples of what the depraved heart of a man can do when there is not an understanding of God's ways. Acts like this cause us to cry out, 'What is our world coming to?'"

Tom Howland
Hope Community Church
Andover, Kansas

"We have been interrupted somehow this week... Evil suddenly showed itself in an attack on New York and Washington D.C... and possibly an attack was planned in other areas in the country. Evil was already there, but it showed itself on Tuesday. Evil showed itself in a very terrible way and we don't like the looks of it."

Ron Stephens
Peebles Church of God
Peebles, Ohio

Lesson 22: The Why Question "Ain't" Easy to Answer

Another lesson we glean from a study of the response of the Church of God to the September 11th terrorist strikes is that the "Why?" question isn't an easy one to answer.

Asking Why?

Uncertainty and fear visited the citizens of this nation in the days following the September 11, 2001 terrorist strikes. We, who had long counted on the security provided by two large oceans which separate our nation from its nearest enemy, woke up on that beautiful fall day to the awful realization that we in this country also are vulnerable to attack.

When tragedy strikes the foundation of an individual life, it too is often shaken to the very core. When a person's health fails or when a key relationship goes bad, the subsequent uncertainty can bring some dark and desperate times. When those pillars or supporting structures of one's life are shaken, individually or collectively, as they were on September 11th, the questions come fast and furious.

In his message on the Sunday after the terrorists attacks, Ancil Abney of Bradenton, Florida, shared with his congregation about how tragedy, like the one that occurred on September 11th, or like the one recorded in the Old Testament book of Job often cause us to ask hard questions.

"A lot of questions confront us, and few answers are available. As I watched television, and listened to the radio, and as I have spoke with people in the community, and in the neighborhood.... I've been struck by the questions that were asked. Without telling one another what we were asking, we all seemed to be asking some of the same questions...Genesis, the first book of the Bible, only has 160 questions...Matthew, the first book of the New Testament, has around 180 questions from beginning to end...The book of Psalms, with its 150 chapters, only asks 160 questions...But the book of Job, forty-two short chapters, asks 330 questions. So, the question may be asked, 'Why does the book of Job have so many more questions than the others?' The answer is simple; it is because the book of Job deals with a horrible, horrible tragedy. Tragedies cause us to ask questions."[104]

---

[104] Ancil Abney. Bradenton, Florida. September 16, 2001.

Dr. Rita Johnson, from Belleville, Michigan, titled her message for the Sunday morning following the terrorist strikes on the United States, "Making Sense of the Senseless." During the days following September 11th, many around this nation were trying to figure out why God, if in fact there was a God, would allow a tragedy of this magnitude to occur. The same confusion develops in the life of the individual facing a personal tragedy. Only days before beginning the first draft of this chapter, I was seated with a family in the waiting room of an ICU unit. A middle-aged woman lay in a coma, unresponsive, attached to life support. Hours before, without warning, she had suffered a massive aneurysm of the brain. Her sister sat with tear stained cheeks, this question on her lips, "Why?" The "why" question isn't an easy question to answer.

"Why" questions are difficult to answer following a tragedy for at least two reasons. First, because the complete answer to the "why" question cannot be known this side of eternity. As the Apostle Paul wrote in I Corinthians 13:11, "For now we see in a mirror dimly." Consider the story of the man whose name was Job, a story many of the movement's ministers across the country preached from on the Sunday following the tragedy, in order to help their congregations gain some insight about how to handle the worst kind of tragedies life forces on us. The book of Job serves as a classic example of the Old Testament's non-traditional wisdom literature. What is the difference between a traditional and non-traditional wisdom source you may ask? A traditional wisdom passage found in the Old Testament Book of Proverbs tells us that if we do right, good things will follow.[105] This may be true, but only to a certain extent. Job, as well as other Old Testament non-traditional wisdom passages, seem to offer a corrective to the traditional "do good and you will be blessed" mentality, lest this thinking go to seed. The problem, of course, with a simple formula of cause and effect like the one outlined in traditional wisdom source material is that we can see many obvious exceptions. The troublemaker is the one who is promoted at the office and ends up

---

[105] J. Benton White, From Adam to Armageddon: a survey of the Bible. 3rd Edition (Belmont, California: Wadsworth Publishing Company, 1994), pp. 87-92

wining the lottery. On the other hand, the most giving and kind of your neighbors is the one laid off and forced to declare bankruptcy. These types of events seem to make no sense. In the Old Testament book of Job we have a story of a man of impeccable moral character, and yet he is visited by one of the most horrific personal tragedies recorded in the Bible. Consider his story:

"Now it happened on the day when his sons and his daughters were eating and drinking wine in their oldest brother's house., that a messenger came to Job and said, 'The oxen were plowing and the donkeys feeding beside them, and the Sabeans attacked and took them. They also slew the servants with the edge of the sword, and I alone have escaped to tell you.' While he was still speaking, another also came and said, 'The fire of God fell from heaven and burned up the sheep and the servants and consumed them, and I alone have escaped to tell you.' While he was still speaking, another also came and said, 'The Chaldeans formed three bands and made a raid on the camels and took them and slew the servants with the edge of the sword; and I alone have escaped to tell you.' While he was still speaking another also came and said, 'Your sons and your daughters were eating and drinking wine in their eldest brother's house, and behold, a great wind came form across the wilderness and struck the four corners of the house, and it fell on the young people and they died; and I alone have escaped to tell you.' Then Job arose and tore his robe and shaved his head, and he fell to the ground and worshipped. He said, 'Naked I came from my mother's womb, and naked I shall return there. The Lord gave and the Lord has taken away. Blessed be the name of the Lord.'" [106]

In the story of Job, we find that this righteous man, though he suffered unspeakable tragedies, one after the other, was able, yet, to stand firm and strong, committed to his faith in God even when the events of his life made no sense to him at all. The type of steadiness and resolve demonstrated by Job in the face of tragedy seemed to be

---

[106] Job 1:13-21.

the virtue many sought to emulate during the dark days following the September 11th terrorist strikes.

A second reason the "why" question is difficult to answer, is that even if there was an discernable answer to this question available to us this side of eternity, we might find that the "why" question might implicate us or someone we love in the making of a particular tragedy. The pain of a marriage gone bad may lead one back to the realization that the marriage was ill advised from the beginning, or that the relationship was doomed because the abandoned spouse was exceedingly self centered or abusive. Or perhaps the "why" question may lead an individual facing vehicular homicide charges to the awful realization that it was their own negligence which caused the fatal car crash. A grieving parent may have to consider that their child met its untimely death because he or she was not properly supervised. It is important to note that even in the above cases, God will of course forgive, and help us, even if the "why" question exposes our own culpability in the making of a tragedy. The fact remains, all of us are imperfect people with limitations it is impossible to always have the foresight and strength to circumvent the making of a tragedy.

On the "Sunday After," generally speaking, people around this nation were in no mood to discuss the culpability this nation may have shared in the September 11th terrorist attacks against the United States. Is our country too one-sided in its support of Israel vis-à-vis the Palestinian cause? Should we have been so vigilant in our efforts to starve Saddam Hussein out of power in the years following the Gulf War? Should troops continue to be stationed in Saudi Arabia given the cultural realities of this very pious Muslim nation? [107]

---

[107] Some in the Arab world believe that this nation's support of Israel discounts the Palestinian people's cry for justice and equality. Politics is not my forte'. I will say that if the Church of God Reformation Movement does believe that the church is now the "spiritual Israel;" She is in a unique position in the Evangelical World. Without fear of incurring the wrath of God by "touching the Lord's anointed," She should raise her timid voice, demanding that Israel honor its sacred Scripture, and behave with mercy and grace toward the Palestinians. There is more than just "an eye for an eye" in the Hebrew Scriptures.

Following the attacks of September 11th, some ministers had the courage to point out the fact that America had created some of her enemies because of its misguided policies around the world.

On the Sunday after the September 11th terrorist strikes Dr. Rita Johnson shared the following comments:

"Let me just stop here and say, that I know that while we are lauding and applauding our country, and we are proud of America, beloved, there are some atrocities that have been committed by the Americans in foreign countries. There is some suffering that has taken place at the hands of our government. We need to understand that. Sometimes...one of God's superior motives is...that the sins of our forefathers would be visited on the generations following...I know that we don't like to hear that, because we like to believe in America. We like to believe that we are lily white, our hands are always clean, but I know that you have heard some things that have shocked you sometimes; things our government has done in foreign countries. [Yes,] even in our own country. Some of the tests that were secretive have only been pulled out later... So, I say that to say that when the Bible says if you suffer, it should not be as a murderer, or thief, or any other kind of criminal, or even a meddler. However, if you suffer as a Christian, do not be ashamed, but praise God that you bear that name. 'For it is time for judgment to begin with the family of God. If it begins with us.' How long have we said, we are the family of God as a nation because we have said, 'In God we trust.'? While we have said that with our lips, our nation, our values, our moral standards have steadily been declining. While we say, we are a [country] that trusts in God, if you really look at some of the things that have happened in our nation, it would be very hard for those who look [from] the outside to say that this is a nation that genuinely trusts in God. We need to be mindful of that." [108]

Randall Spence, from Springfield, Ohio, goes so far as to suggest that asking the "why" question may not yield a suitable answer. He

---

[108] Dr. Rita Johnson. "Making Sense Out of the Senseless." Belleville, Michigan. September 16, 2001.

suggests that it may be more fruitful during times of tragedy to simply trust in God. The focus for perseverance in tragedy, according to Spence, then moves from knowing why, to knowing God. He made the following comments in his message entitled "Why?":

"The bottom line is, some questions in life we are simply not intended to understand. And one of them happens to be the question, 'why?' Ultimately consolation is not found in knowing the answer to 'why'? But rather in knowing God... I have said over the last number of weeks, that if we asked the wrong question we sometimes will get the wrong answer. The wrong question happens to be, 'Why does evil seem to prosper?' But the right question is, 'In whom do I find my comfort in the midst of the evil that surrounds me? When the world comes tumbling in on top of me, in whom will I find my comfort and my consolation and my peace?' Yes, there are some things in life we simply will never understand...in chapter two, verse four of Habakkuk, God gives us the answer that we seek. He says, 'The righteous will live by their faith.' When we do not understand what is going on around us, when we do not understand God's ways, even when we find [His ways] almost impossible to accept, the answer is, trust in God."[109]

Lesson 23: Tragedy Happens Because Satan And Evil Are Active In This World

Tragedy happens because evil and its chief proponent, Satan, leaves a swathe of unspeakable destruction in every life in which he is given even a toe hold, and in every place where evil is given a host.

Evil, And the Work of Satan

One of the explanations given in pulpits September 16th as to why this tragedy occurred was that it occurred because our enemy was carrying out his agenda of death and destruction. It would have been

---

[109] Randall Spence. "Why." Springfield, Ohio. September 23, 2001.

difficult to have not noticed the fingerprints of Satan and his evil cronies in the heartless terrorist strikes. [110]

In John 10:10, Jesus reminded His followers that He had come to give them "abundant" life, but that the thief, or the evil one, Satan, comes only "to steal, and kill, and to destroy;" I Peter 5:8 compares the evil one to a "roaring lion."

From these two scriptural texts it is apparent that we have an enemy that is bent on destroying all that is good in this world; our relationships, our health, our very lives.

A number of ministers across the movement were able to make some sense out of the catastrophe of the events of September 11th, by explaining that, evil, sin and Satan were responsible. The kingdom of darkness, it was explained, had an agenda of death and destruction and so carried it out through the individual sinful acts of a number of hijackers.

In my own message I shared the following insights:

"This week we came face to face with a manifestation of abject evil … Planes crashing … horrific explosions … people jumping from buildings, cries and screams. Thousands were murdered, sirens in the streets, military jets in the skies ... Countless Tears … 'Sin thrived.' Where sin lives and thrives I don't want to be…where hatred, prejudice, lust and greed are given free reign…that place becomes uninhabitable—a smoldering hell."[111]

---

[110] It may be helpful at this point to give a very elementary definition of these terms, "evil, sin, Satan."

1.) Evil may be defined as anything that is outside of the domain of God, any act, attitude, thought that is anti- God, anti- love, anti- light, anti- life, anti- peace.

2.) Sin may be defined as any specific act, attitude or thought perpetrated by an individual that is wittingly or unwittingly motivated by the forces of evil.

3.) Satan or the devil can be identified as the leader of the kingdom of evil, as the antithesis of God, right, and good.

[111] Gary Agee. "Tragedy and Triumph." West Chester, Ohio. September 16, 2001.

Jim Lyon from Anderson, Indiana, speaks of the evil force at work in our world evidenced by the events of September 11th:

"Make no mistake about it, even as we worship and honor our great and good God, there is another force, there is another personality, who is at work in our world. In fact, this personality is very powerful. His power must not intimidate us, but we must respect it just the same. This person is Satan, of course. Shrouded in mystery, we're not sure of [evil's] origins; we're not sure exactly how [Satan] functions. But we know this, he is the antithesis, the opposite of God. When God seeks wholeness, Satan seeks brokenness. When God revels in righteous joy, Satan revels in desperate sadness. In the Bible, Satan is a word which means adversary...You may often hear me say, once again dramatically proved to you before your eyes this week, there is a heaven, and there is a hell. There is a God; there is a Satan; there is a right; there is a wrong. There is a future with God, and there is a future with Satan. The [future with God] will be bright and complete; the [future with Satan] is doomed. We will decide upon which course we pursue. Satan is the adversary. He is revealed to us in the Old Testament. There are many, many Scriptures in the Old Testament that give us a glimpse of who he is. But [Satan] is most completely disclosed in the New Testament... Jesus, in fact, is the one voice in all of history who has given us the most information about Satan. Jesus called him the 'prince of this world.' In that, Jesus was reminding us that this world, created perfect by God, had been stolen from God's hands, by the devil himself. He is the prince of this world, he has a foothold of power in this world. And the conflict in this country is the attempt by heaven to redeem the world from the grasp of Satan, to restore to God what has been stolen by him. He is the prince of this world, and he has tremendous power to wreak havoc in the world in which we live. But make no mistake about it, Jesus came into this world, according to John the Apostle who witnessed it with his own eyes, that He might destroy the works of the devil. You see that? Jesus entered into this world, and ever since He came, He has been about the business of destroying, one by one, the works of the devil. Satan is raging about it. Satan knows that if the Lord prevails he is doomed. Satan knows that he has to fight back, and he is desperate. These outrageous crimes that we have witnessed...are the despicable evil, the President described. These acts are simply the evidence of hell's rage against heaven. Jesus, however, has come to destroy the works of the devil, and the devil is feeling the heat; he's feeling the pressure. We need to be sure we keep the pressure on." [112]

Rolland Daniels from Clayton, Ohio, stated it this way in his message to his congregation Sunday morning, September 16:

"Why did God let this happen? You want to know something? Never before in the history of this country... have you and I... seen an illustration of the consequences of the falleness of man like we did on Tuesday... Know with the falleness of man... there were consequences... We had good, and we had evil. You and I have just recognized and witnessed one of the sickest displays of evil on the face of the earth. God is not up top pulling some numbers saying 'Think I'm going to let some airliners fly into the World Trade Center today.' Don't think that for a moment. We have seen the devastation the tragedy and the sickness of evil. The most amazing thing is that in the midst of great evil, God comes so powerfully, God comes so magnificently, and He brings good even to evil." [113]

Paul Dreger from Goshen, Indiana, shared the following with his flock the Sunday after the terrorist strikes against the United States:

"How could such a thing happen? Such a thing could happen because we live in a world infiltrated by sin. There is no other explanation for what took place on Tuesday September 11, 2001, than the fact that sin is at work in our world today. Jesus warned His followers that in this world they would face tribulation, they would face difficulty; they persecuted Me; they will persecute you. Jesus himself was crucified on the cross of Calvary. Because of the presence of sin in the world, He suffered and bled and died. Death is the result of sin. God chose us for life." [114]

---

[112] Jim Lyon. "Bad Spirit Removed." Anderson, Indiana. September 16, 2001.

[113] Rolland Daniels. " God is." Clayton, Ohio. September 16, 2001.

[114] Paul Dreger. Goshen, Indiana. September 16, 2001.

Lesson 24: The Believer In Christ Can Overcome Evil

Overcoming Evil

Evil is very much a reality in this world. The result of the savagery, lust and prejudice springing from evil are daily spread across newspapers all over the world. But though evil and its ugly results are all too real in this world, there are some things we can do to overcome these forces in our lives.

In my own message delivered on September 16, 2001, I point out that often times evil results from choices made by the individuals in direct violation of the directives from the Bible:

"It is our rebellion against God that causes pockets of hell on this earth. It behooves us to 'rid evil from the world.' Evil takes many forms, bombings, hijackings, greed, lust, indifference, pride and prejudice. If we are honest, evil is not merely outside…in the life of the terrorist, it is also manifested on the inside of every person. Let us overcome evil in our own lives with good…Commit to reading God's Word: applying it to your life, obeying it. Allow God to work in your life."[115]

The following is a list of suggestions that I hope might prove helpful in overcoming the power of evil in your life:

1.) Familiarize yourself with God's Word. Read it and let the values, truths and directives guide your thinking and your actions.

2.) Pray regularly for God's direction in your life.

3.) Attend worship and establish accountability with likeminded believers.

---

[115] Gary Agee. Tragedy and Triumph. West Chester, Ohio. September 16, 2001.

4.)   Understand that God is at work making you to be an overcomer.

Lesson 25: God Is Always Working To Bring Good Out Of The Evil Active In This World

Jesus, in John 16:33, promises His disciples that they will have trouble in this world. He goes on to say that they are not to worry because He has overcome the world. As Christians, we believe that evil has been defeated. We hold to the conviction that we are living through the working out of the defeat of evil, a defeat that was sealed and signed on the day Jesus rose from the dead. As followers of Christ, Christians too are called to be overcomers. It is in our genetic makeup. Jesus conquered His most pernicious enemy, death. We also have an unclaimed victory over this, our archenemy. Having said this, we are called to subdue all of our lesser enemies as well. We are called to overcome evil. One of the ways we are able to overcome evil, and the demoralizing effect it has in our lives, is to recognize that God is at work in each tragedy that visits the life of the believer. Romans 8:28 says:

"And we know that God causes all things to work together for good to those who love God, to those who are called according to His purpose."

Again, in my own message on September 16th, I attempt to explain how God was involved in turning Christianity's darkest tragedy in a redemptive direction. In this portion of my sermon I discuss the crucifixion of Jesus, and God's awesome hand in the turning of that tragedy into triumph.

"We know that darkness can't stand against the light. Yes, darkness had its day. But, God is working. I am reminded of the crucifixion story…. The disciples watched violent hands take their Lord and best friend, put Him up on the tree, and murder this innocent person. That for them was the darkest day of their lives. And what did God do? He took that situation, that was so desperate, and hopeless, and He took that event and turned it around; God raised Jesus from the dead. And all of us have a hope, even in the darkest day."

"I have decided that I don't want God's job. I've decided that I don't want it at all. Part of the reason I don't want His job, is because it is just too hard. Part of the reason I don't want God's job is that it is just too much. Now, I complain once in a while that I am very busy. I've got this class to teach, and this class to prepare for, and Sunday School and a Bible Study and I've got my kids...But I want you to understand that God is constantly doing exactly what He is doing in this passage; He is cleaning up our messes...He promised, 'That all things work together for the good to those who love God, and to those who are called according to His purpose.' So, I imagine Him as a pilot of a great ship....the bombs exploding. Yet He takes that situation and turns it to the good. I can imagine Him over and over in countless millions and billions of lives, taking all the that is wrought one against the other....all the violence, all the prejudice, and all the relational problems and steering every one of those hard to the right. And turning those things toward the good...This is the kind of Heavenly Father that we serve." [116]

The believer can know with the assurance of God's Word that God is working to turn tragedy to the good. As a number of ministers pointed out on the Sunday after the terrorist attacks on the United States, rescue workers and a hoard of volunteers risking life and limb rushed toward the same places where evil had left its ugly scars. People from all walks of life, motivated by love for God and their fellow citizens, cared for the victims. They prayed and counseled with the survivors, and they gave in record amounts in order that the families of the victims might be cared for. God was at work turning tragedy into triumph.

The "Why" Question, Theodicy And Free Will

---

[116] Ibid.

In the Christian community, there is a dilemma in our theology that isn't easy to sort out. The events of September 11th brought that dilemma to the fore, as does every personal tragedy experienced in the lives of individuals. The dilemma, is known as the theodicy question. It can be explained as follows: If God is all powerful, which many Christians believe that He is, And if God is all loving, which Christians say that He is, then why does He permit violent acts to occur, people to become victims of tragedy, when He knows that unbelievable grief and pain will follow?

Randall Spence attempted to address this question in his message entitled simply, "Why."

"We all watched with horror the planes being flown into the twin towers of the World Trade Center in New York. I am sure that among other questions, the one primary question that we all asked is, 'Why?' Whenever tragedy strikes we always find ourselves asking this particular question. Why do such senseless things take place? Why does God allow such evil to exist? [Why does He allow] evil men seemingly to prosper? That is the question I want to seek to give some answer to this morning. I must say to preface my statement, that the answer I give is an academic [answer.] It doesn't really respond to the heart so much. But, hopefully, as we begin to understand [this answer] on an intellectual level, on a logical level, perhaps it will help us with the feelings that we have as well. When you come to life's biggest questions, the one question that seems to loom above all the others is the so called 'theodicy question.' The question in essence can be summed up as follows: 'If God is good, if He is just, if He is loving, and He is all powerful, then why does He allow the existence of pain, suffering and evil in our world?' Essentially there are two explanations that I share with you just in summary fashion this morning as to why bad things happen. The first, and perhaps most obvious, is because of Natural Law. When God created the universe, He created certain laws of the universe in order to keep the universe working consistently. An example would be the Law of Gravity. The Law of Gravity is our friend, in that if it were not for the Law of Gravity we all would be floating off into space. But break the Law of Gravity, and it can kill you. Jump off the side of a building…gravity will kill you. Gravity is on one hand our friend, on the other; it can be our enemy. You see the reality is that we do not break the laws of nature; they break us when we go against them. There is a second reason why bad things happen...because of human freedom. You see the reality is that when God created us human creatures, He chose to give us a free will. We might ask, 'Why? Why would God make that choice?' For this very reason, because God in His very essence is love... God is love. Love mandated that He give us free will. That means that you and I have a free choice whether we will love Him and serve Him, or whether we will reject Him and curse Him. We make that choice! It is called free will. Were God to have made us in such a fashion where we had to serve Him and had to love Him, we would not be free agents. We would be robots instead. You know, and I know that love is not something that can be forced, it cannot be dictated, it cannot be mandated. I cannot say to my wife, you will love me! Love is a choice; it is a decision...God is Love! And love mandated that He give us human creatures the free choice whether or not we will love Him or despise Him...God allows evil because God's essential quality is love. Since He is love, love required that He give us free will. And in giving us free will, He had to allow the consequences of our choices. That means that I have the right, as a free will agent, to come up and stick a gun in your face, and I can choose to kill you. Now is that God's will? Of course not! But, God has to allow it to happen...Were God to stop, step in, and prevent that person who has jumped out of a building from hitting the ground and killing themselves, He would be breaking the very law of nature that He has set into place. And if He were to likewise step in and cause me not to do what I choose to do, He would be breaking the natural law that He has put into place.... So much of the suffering that we see in our world today, especially the suffering that we are experiencing now as a people, as a nation, as a world community is a result of people making bad choices, people making choices to harm, to hurt others as we have seen in this recent tragedy. I might add, [another] reason why God allows tragedy to take place, that I have not listed on the outline...is to bring us back to Him...[117] That

---

[117] Randall Spence clearly articulates, as many others did in their September 16th

is one of the things that we see seemingly happening, at least on a temporary basis in our nation. Whenever Israel's enemies overtook them, whenever Israel was attacked in some fashion, was threatened in some respect, God used that occasion to draw her back to Him. I believe that in like fashion... God will use this tragedy to bring us as a people back to the principles on which this nation was founded. Let's make 'in God we trust' more than something that we simply put ...on our money. Let's go back to the essentials, upon which this nation was founded. And truly be a people who trust in God. Well, there are two essential kinds of suffering somewhat in summation that I would share. Tragedy caused by natural calamity, disease, earthquakes, tornadoes, hurricanes would be examples. The second kind of suffering is that which is the result of human choice. [118] If some terrorist chooses to hijack a plane and to fly it into the World Trade Center, countless families reap the consequences of that choice. Is it fair? Heavens no, it is not fair. But, that is the consequence of free choice. During World War II, Hitler chose to try to exterminate the Jewish race. He succeeded in eliminating some six million Jews. During that same era, Joseph Stalin killed... more people than Hitler; most of them were his own people, the people of the Soviet Union. In 1949, Communism took over China. During the reign of Mao Tse Tung...an estimated ninety million people were killed. Was it fair? Of course not! One of the essential realities that we need to embrace is the reality that life isn't fair. God has never promised us that life would be equitable. He has never promised us that life would seem fair. You see, the thing that we need to embrace as a people of faith is that fairness is a promise of eternity not a promise of earth. For in this present realm Satan rules, if you will. He is the Lord of this earth. As

---

messages, that God did not cause the events of September 11th to occur. Instead, He permitted them to occur in order that individuals would return to God.

[118] Randall Spence was the only minister surveyed who attempted to address the theodicy in a more intellectual fashion. I appreciated his efforts. I do find it curious that he is the only surveyed minister to mention the issue of natural calamity in their respective messages. When there is someone to blame, as was the case in the September 11th tragedy, it seems much easier to "let God off the hook." It is much harder, in my view, to portray God as loving in the wake of an F5 tornado or a Category 5 hurricane.

long as Satan is alive, as long as Satan exists fairness will not be a part of this earth."[119]

Lesson 26: God's Will Is Not Always Done In This World

Stephen Birch, of Lexington, Kentucky, addresses a number of related issues in his message the Sunday after the September 11th terrorist strikes. He points out that cause and effect is not always effective when explaining why tragedy visits one's life. In his message, he cites the Luke 13 passage that describes Jesus' explanation of two well-known first century tragedies. The first was a massacre carried out in the temple by Pilate the governor of the region; the second was the collapse of a tower in Siloam, which killed eighteen people. Birch points out that though God could have stopped the planes from hitting the World Trade Center and the Pentagon this would have been in effect a violation of His commitment to our free will. He also suggests, in this message that the will of God is not always done on this earth.

Lesson 27: Tragedy Happens Because People Exercise Their Choice To Do Evil

Stephen Birch offered the following comments:

"The Bible teaches us that this is not a perfect world. This is a world of sin and wrongdoing that results in human suffering. The Bible pulls no punches about this truth. Listen to Ecclesiastes 8:14, 'Sometimes something useless happens on earth. Bad things happen to good people. And good things happen to bad people.' What is he saying? He is saying we do not always get what we deserve. There are two mistakes that we sometimes make when it comes to this whole area of tragedy in life... One is to believe that when good things happen to me, this means I am good. And when bad things happen to me, that means I am bad. That is wrong. In Luke chapter thirteen,

---

[119] Randall Spence. "Why." Springfield, Ohio. September 16, 2001.

Jesus is talking about two tragedies that occurred in His day. Jesus, the Son of God, was also aware of disaster and tragedies in life. He says, you know, there were a bunch of folks worshipping in the temple and they were brutally murdered. Do you recall the tower that fell on eighteen people and killed them? Jesus asked this question, 'Who sinned that caused this tragedy?' Was this the result...of their sin? Jesus answers His own question. No, Absolutely not! Now, this does not negate the effects of cause and effect. The truth is, most of the problems that occur in our lives are our own fault, the results of things we do or don't do. If you drive too fast on bald tires, you can have a blow out and a have a serious accident. If you drink and drive, you can cause great calamity to yourself and to others. If we eat too much, our blood pressure gets too high. And if we don't take care of ourselves physically, we can suffer heart attacks and strokes. We do reap what we sow, but not always. Sometimes we suffer innocently...Not everything that happens to you is the will of God. When I hear people at funerals make statements like this, 'Well it must have just been their time.' 'Well, it must have just been God's will.'...That is not true. Don't blame God for Columbine High School. Don't blame God for the disaster at the World Trade Center. Could God have stopped those terrorists? Well, let me think. God created the world. He made the universe. He made galaxies so far away that we are just now getting telescopes that we can even know that they are there. He made life so complex that we are just beginning to understand a little bit about it. Do you think God could have stopped an airplane? Well, probably so. All He had to do to stop that airplane was to take away their free will, their freedom to choose. But if He took away the free will of the terrorist pilots, He would also have to remove our free will, our greatest blessing...It is also our greatest curse, because often we choose poorly. When we choose, wrong people suffer. Do you understand this? God's will is not always done on this earth. If you don't believe that just listen to what he says in 2 Peter 3:9. He says, 'It is God's will that all should repent. And that none should perish.' Let me ask you, do all repent? No. Do some perish? Yes. Why? Because God will never force His will on our will. God will never make you do something by forcing His will on you. In a little while, we will have an invitation for people to accept Christ. He won't make you do that. He will give you the invitation. He will give you the opportunity to say yes to His love; He will not force His love on you. The Revelation says He stands at the door and knocks. He doesn't kick the door in. He just knocks. We have the freedom to say yes and to say, no. With that freedom comes the possibility of tragedy and pain. That is why in the Lord's Prayer we pray these words: 'Thy will be done on earth as it is in heaven.' Why? Because God's will is not always done on earth as it is in heaven. How is it done in heaven? It is done perfectly. We pray, just as Your will is done perfectly in heaven, we would love for that to happen here on earth. If that were already true there would be no need to pray. It is not always done here perfectly on earth."[120]

Wayne Putman from Dallas, Texas, picking up some of the same themes, made the following comments in his September 16 message:

"He could have stopped the terrorists. God could have intervened and kept those planes form doing the damage that they did. But in order for Him to do that He would have had to taken away the freedom to choose, freedom that He gave every single one of us. And if He took it away from those terrorists, He would also have to take it away from us. We would, then, simply become robots at His beckoned will and call and not have that precious free will that He has given to us. He has given each of us freedom to choose. Apart from Him people choose wrong. So, what that means is that God's will is not always done in the world."[121]

I spoke, in my September 16th message, to the role of free will in the tragedy of September 11th as it related to the hijackers:

"I want to remind you again as I said before, God gives us the freedom to choose. Let's not blame everything on Him. When we walk away from Him, when we choose to go against His word, there are consequences. People get hurt. The reason God gives us a set of commands is because He loves us. And walking outside those

---

[120] Stephen Birch. Lexington, Kentucky. September 16, 2001.
[121] Wayne Putman. "Recovering From Lives Disasters." Dallas, Texas. September 16, 2001.

110

boundaries has terrible ramifications, in our individual lives and also in the lives of those that we love. God gave freedom, and people chose the evil. And so evil was compounded over and over again. And the tears in people's lives were spread all over the place."[122]

Dave Colp from Middletown, Ohio, discusses how the freedom of choice lead to the terrorist strikes of September 11th:

"The first thing I would share with you, is that there is a cost to freedom. Sin has consequences, death, disease and destruction. These entered the world through sin. God told Adam and Eve in the garden, 'that if you sin, if you eat from this one tree, you will surely die.' They disobeyed, and the result was there was a spiritual death; the relationship they enjoyed with God the Father in the garden was broken; it was severed. They were cast out of the garden; they were cut off. That disobedience, that sin, also caused death in a physical way, because death entered the world through their sin… There is a penalty that comes with that kind of freedom. Our nation is paying the tab for that freedom. There is cost all over our world. There are repercussions all over this world as a result of those who chose to ignore God, that chose to ignore what is right, that chose to ignore what was moral, and chose to decide what was right in their own eyes, in their own mind. And that friends is the cost of freedom. And our nation on Tuesday, paid the cost of freedom….We paid the cost of the sin of another…People sin, and the consequences are paid in the lives of those that surround them, and the ripple effect goes out from there…Sin does not happen in a vacuum…. The sin affected more than just the eighteen or nineteen hijackers and those who had helped them organize this event. This sin has affected the entire world…"[123]

---

[122] Gary Agee. "Tragedy and Triumph." West Chester, Ohio. September 16, 2001. It should be noted that many people on September 11th and in the days following exercised their free choice in incredibly noble and caring ways. Let us not minimize the individual choices made by the many rescue workers who chose to risk their own lives in order to save others. Some who exercised their free will in this manner made the ultimate sacrifice.

[123] Dave Colp. "911, God, God are you There?" Middletown, Ohio. September 16, 2001.

Though the "why" question doesn't always seem easy to answer, it is productive to ask it, if only because it has the potential of leading us into a season of reflection. This period of reflection and prayer may lead to the discovery of changes in behavior that might minimize the pain of tragedy in one's life. From this chapter, we discovered that the explanations for why the devastating attacks of September 11th occurred had to do with the presence of evil in the life of not only the terrorist, but also in the life of every person. By working to eliminate evil from our lives, we, in fact, are well on our way to defeating evil in the world. For evil is reigned in only when individuals choose life; when they choose to no longer loan their mind, bodies, and souls to evil's crusade of death and destruction. Also in this chapter, it is apparent that many of the ministers who participated in this study believed that the exercising of one's own free will was a huge factor in this tragedy. In this particular event, it was the free will exercised by thirteen men who chose to be agents of evil resulting in the death of over three thousand people. It is my desire that the insights from this section would create in you a desire to exercise your free will in caring and loving ways that will in turn positively impact many people. Let us now move to the next lesson where we will discuss fear, faith and hope as we continue to examine what lessons and insights we might gain in order to better face our own personal tragedies.

Chapter Five Questions For Discussion

1.) Following the terrorist strikes of September 11th, how frequently did the why question come up with friends and colleagues? How did you respond? Explain your response.

2.) Free choice exercised in a way displeasing to God was one of the main reasons given for the tragedy of September 11th. Were there others?

3.) The author gives four suggestions as to how to overcome evil and its negative effects in your life. Give two more. Why did you choose these?

4.) Pick up a copy of your local newspaper. From the articles, highlight individuals who have made good moral choices. Next list some poor moral choices. Discuss how you determined which was a good and which was an evil moral choice.

5.) What role do the following agencies play in removing evil from the world: Federal Government, Children Services, Schools, Armed forces, Federal, State and local law enforcement?

6.) Identify in your community some of the positive results of September 11th. Do you see God's hand in these outcomes? Explain.

7.) Have there been changes in your moral choices since September 11th? Explain.

Chapter Six
Take Courage!

"If you think that the horrific, evil acts being planned have come to an end, you are seriously mistaken. The terrorists will be encouraged by their modicum of success to launch out all the more vigorously. That is not to cause us to be fearful, but it is to cause us to take seriously the need for the saints of God to be in the place of fasting and prayer, to call upon God to rescue us from our enemies."

Tony Cunningham
Radiant Life Church
Sacramento, California

Lesson 28: Tragedy Can Make Us Afraid

As the horrible events of September 11th began to sink into the minds of Americans, an overwhelming sense of fear and uncertainty was born and then spread rapidly across this nation like a rogue wave. Never before in the history of the United States of America, had an enemy been able to so stealthily and successfully strike down so many innocent unsuspecting people. The terrorist strikes were truly a tragedy of epic proportions. Following the strikes, there was the sense that if this disciplined group of hijackers could simultaneously hijack airliners and in three out of four cases hit major U.S. symbols of wealth and power, then what else were they capable of? The questions were many at that time. People wondered if there were other terrorist cells in the United States at the time, waiting for just the right moment to make another deadly attack on the citizens of this nation. People also wondered whether the terrorists might try to commandeer other airliners and crash them. Speculation about where the terrorists would strike next whipped the country into a panic. Would they strike the subway system with so many being transported daily from destination to destination? Would this network of terrorists use a chemical or biological agent capable of killing large numbers of people? Had these terrorists secured nuclear materials enabling them to explode a dirty nuclear bomb at major sporting events where there might be as many as fifty thousand gathered?

Add to this the anthrax scare that occurred not long after the attacks on the World Trade Center, which initially seemed to be just another method the terrorists were employing in order to kill and to create panic. The first of these biological attacks was apparently directed at Senator Tom Daschel. Tragically, postal workers died of anthrax exposure. Congressional office buildings were shut down for fear that another attack would occur. Mail was checked and screened. It seems bizarre in retrospect, but people were very afraid to open their mail for fear of coming into contact with anthrax spores.

On Halloween, media outlets were reporting that there had been traces of anthrax discovered in a postal machine in Indianapolis. When I heard the news, I felt fear well inside me. For this book, I had received a number of tapes for review from around the country. Some of those tapes came from the state of Indiana. I believed, at this time, that they most likely came through the post office in Indianapolis. I thought about my own well being and the well being of my administrative assistant. Was I endangering the lives of my family? In hindsight, my fears seem so exaggerated. Suffice it to say, at the time they seemed genuine. [124] As if the relatively few cases of people being exposed to the deadly anthrax spores weren't bad enough, the anthrax incidents set off a wave of copy cat attacks. People packed baby powder or baking soda into letters and mailed them in order to settle scores with a lover or an enemy, adding to the atmosphere of fear which hung like a dark cloud over this country following the terrorist attacks of September 11th.

This sense of fear was widespread. Even pastors and religious leaders across the Church of God Movement confessed to being fearful and anxious over the events that had taken place.

---

[124] Initial press reports suggested that anthrax had been discovered in postal machines near Indianapolis. It was later reported, however, that these machines were not being used to process mail, but were rather being cleaned for an out of state client on the east coast.

116

Consider the comments made after the attacks by Stephen Weldon from Andover, Kansas:

"I cannot tell you that I am not personally struggling with all that has transpired since September 11th. I cannot tell you that I have not, and do not, have my own fears and concerns. I cannot tell you that I have been worry free...I cannot stand before you and state that everything is going to be all right; to utter such words would be a lie. After all, we live on a sinful planet where there are many evil people. I will not lie to you by telling you that everything will be fine or that we will not experience any more senseless and violent bloodshed. I will not stand before you as the false prophets of Jeremiah's day who, we are told in Jeremiah 6:14, 'dressed the wound of the people as though it were not serious; peace, peace they said when there was no peace.' But I can stand before you with great confidence and joy and tell you that in the long run, if you trust in God through Christ, I can tell you it is going to be all right. I can tell you we win in the end. I can tell you that God is our strong tower, and He will conquer all evil. I can tell you we will dwell with God forever in a perfect place. I can tell you there is hope, and a reason for living. And I can tell you as an ambassador of Jesus that, we are needed now more than ever in this sinful and dying world." [125]

Raymond Chin, from Chicago, Illinois, described the state of fear that had pervaded the nation following the assault on the Pentagon and the World Trade Center September 11th:

"Events we never thought we would see; events that we never thought would happen here, have shattered the façade of our invincibility, our power and our might, our sense of safety and freedom. It has shattered the American can do [mentality] and American efficiency. We feel we can handle almost anything. We can find a solution to any problem. That is the American can do mentality. But these events have shattered that façade. It is ironic in my mind that even though we have the best armies in the world, we have the most sophisticated computer programs around, we have the most efficient

---

[125] Stephen Weldon. "Strong Tower." Andover, Kansas. September 16, 2001.

117

airplanes, we have the most efficient information gathering agencies any where in the world, most sophisticated ships and submarines, it is amazing that the enemies of good, the purveyors of evil, have awakened our conscious and or emotions; they have used their convictions and simple things like knives… and have done some harm and damage to this country. Even though the events have brought us together in patriotism, if we are honest with ourselves, we need to admit to ourselves that we have lost our innocence. We have lost our sense of security. We have become fearful of today, fearful of tomorrow, afraid of war. Below the surface of our emotions, we have questions that we can't answer. We are dealing with emotions that we can't even interpret or understand ourselves."[126]

Fear and tragedy seem to be traveling companions. When personal tragedy visits the life of the individual, fear and uncertainty seem to come along as unwelcome guests. Take, for example, the life of a middle-aged woman whose husband decides he is no longer in love with her. Fear in this case takes a number of forms; fear of being rejected, fear of being stigmatized and fear of growing old alone. For the father who is the victim of company downsizing, he fears not being able to find work, or having to declare bankruptcy. The fear of an elderly person may be the fear of deteriorating health or the loss of his or her freedom.

Lesson 29: Jesus Came To Give Us The Victory Over Our Fears

No matter what the source of fear, God desires that people live the "abundant life." This life of abundance cannot be realized if one is constantly being tortured and harassed by fear; fear of the past or future, fear of failure, fear of becoming a victim of terror, fear of being injured, fear of being rejected, or the most daunting fear of all, the fear of death itself.

---

[126] Raymond Chin. Chicago, Illinois. September 16, 2001.

In the book of Hebrews, one discovers that the Lord came to defeat the granddaddy of all the fears, the fear of death. The writer of the Hebrews says it this way:

"Since the children share in flesh and blood, He Himself likewise also partook of the same, that through death He might render powerless him who had the power of death, that is, the devil; and might deliver those who through fear of death were subject to slavery all their lives."[127]

The fear of death, according to this biblical text, follows, hassles, badgers and terrorizes us all of our lives. We are hard pressed as humans to escape its shadow of dread. If, however, it was the desire of God to destroy the biggest and most persistent of our fears, it stands to reason that He must also want to destroy all of the lesser fears. Will we be able to meet our bills this month? Will I be accepted at a new school?, Will I have the strength to face the challenges of tomorrow? Hebrews is not the only Biblical book that addresses the issue of fear. Quite a large number of books address the topic of fear. God wants us to overcome our fears.

Many in the Christian community found help and comfort in the words of the immortal passage, Psalm 46, following the tragic events of September 11th. Consider again the words of the first few verses of this chapter:

"God is our refuge and strength, a very present help in trouble. Therefore, we will not fear, though the earth should change, And though the mountains slip into the heart of the sea. Though its waters roar and foam, though the mountains quake at its swelling pride." [128]

What the above text is describing is a major geological event. It is not everyday that we experience a cataclysmic earthquake, or that we witness the mountains crashing into the sea. Yet, the tragedy of September 11, 2001, had the feel of a real earth shaking disaster. Personal tragedies might also be measured on the Richter scale, so to speak. For they are, by their very nature, foundation shaking events.

---

[127] Hebrews 2:14-15.
[128] Psalm 46: 1-3.

The earth, once so immovable and predictable under one's feet, without warning can shift and the mountains can skip away, crashing into the sea. These kinds of seismic events in our lives quite naturally evoke fear as we seek solid footing that will prove firm and trustworthy.

As people flocked into the churches across the country on September 16th, they wanted to have their felt fears addressed.

Paul Mumaw from St. Joseph, Michigan, prior to the celebration of the Lord's Supper, made the following comments about fear and the figurative storm of September 11th:

"Labor Day, Monday, we had a thunderstorm and our four year old was up in his bedroom. We had one of those loud bursts of thunder. He began to cry, so I ran up and got him and carried him downstairs. When he saw Mom he said, 'Oh, there is Mom. She'll say nice things to me.' Last Tuesday, we had a storm of another type. And in the same childlike way we are go to the Lord saying, 'say nice things to us, reassure us of Your love, reassure us of Your provision, and Your protection, and of our eternal salvation with You...' So, these tangible elements that will be passed to you are just that symbols of His love for you." [129]

Moving Into The Future Without Fear

Earl Wheatley, Jr., from Meridian, Mississippi, explains that it is important to move into the future without fear. In his message, the Sunday after the terrorist strikes, he shares the following:

"We need to decide that we do not go to fear. Fear is the ultimate aim of the terrorists. The terrorists understand that they could never defeat our Army, Navy, Air Force or Marines. They understand that. They know that they are out numbered, out gunned and out manned. They know this. As a result, their strategy is to make societies afraid... Every enemy wants us to be afraid...When God speaks to his people in the Bible, the first words His messengers use are, 'Fear not.'

---

[129] Paul Mumaw. St. Joseph, Michigan. September 16, 2001.

120

Whenever we enter into warfare, we also enter into spiritual warfare. And friends I have a belief that when we get to see this past Tuesday replayed in heaven, we are not only going to see an aircraft crashing into the World Trade Center Towers, we are also going to see demonic forces holding the wings of those planes, and helping beginner pilots be able to guide them to their target…This is not just an attack from a mad terrorist, this is a spiritual attack on our nation, and this is why God's Words must speak to us clearly that we, 'Fear not.' We have to remember what David told those near him before he went to go fight against Goliath. He said, 'It is not by sword or spear that the Lord saves, for the battle is the Lord's.' David…understood the battle was the Lord's. The battle our nation is entering and the war that has been declared against terrorism will ultimately be God's war…We must go forward not in fear, but in faith, because faith with wisdom will always defeat fear. Pastor Kay read the most marvelous section from Romans chapter eight. I shared it with the school children across the street when the principal called and asked me to come over and pray. It was so neat to talk with Mr. Kelly before we went in and he said, 'Say whatever you want.'… I shared with the children that 'We are more than conquerors in Jesus Christ. What shall separate us from the love of Christ? Shall trouble or hardship or persecution or famine or nakedness or danger or even the sword. No. In all these things we are more than conquerors through him who loved us.' And Paul tells us what our conviction should also be. 'For I am convinced that neither death nor life neither angels nor demons, neither the present nor the future nor any powers, neither height nor depth, nor any thing else in all creation will be able to separate us from the love of God in Christ Jesus our Lord.' We need to move forward in faith with wisdom to defeat fear."[130]

The Courage Of Jesus

---

[130] Earl Wheatley, Jr. Meridian, Mississippi. September 16, 2001.

Rod Stafford, in his message September 16th, speaks of a young man inspired by the fearlessness of Jesus as He faced death. He shared the following comments:

"Vic said to me that day, he said, 'You know Rod, I have faced death a lot in my life. And I know what it does to a person to truly know that in the next few moments your life may be taken.' Now, Vic had my attention because I had never known that. 'Rod, I have faced that, and I have seen brave, strong patriotic men absolutely paralyzed in fear as they faced the possibility of losing their life.' And he said, 'Even though I was never paralyzed and I was able to keep on fighting, I know the utter terror that I felt facing the possibility in the next moment of having my life ripped away from me.' He said, 'But when I faced death, I faced death fully armed. I had my weapon, and I could do my best to protect myself from anyone who wanted to take my life. And I had something that at least gave me the possibility and in every case gave me the opportunity to take their life before they took mine. I know how frightened I was, even fully armed. And now I read about this man who faced death clothed in nothing but just a seamless little garment, completely unarmed.' And he said to me something to me, you know, I guess I have known but it meant something new to me hearing it from him. He said, 'He must have been scared about what was about to happen.' And then Vic said, 'He did all of that, I realize, for me, to pay for my sins, to make me clean so that I didn't have to experience the consequences of my own sin. The Bible says the wages of sin is death. That is the consequence we ought to pay.' And Vic said, 'Christ did all of that that I would not have to take the consequences for my own sin. He said when I came to realize that, and I came to realize how profound God's love was for me, I wanted to love him back.'"[131]

Lesson 30: The Antidotes To Fear: Are Faith And Hope

For the epidemic of fear that spread across the country following the September 11th terrorist attacks, a number of ministers offered their

---

[131] Rod Stafford. Fairfax, Virginia. September 16, 2001.

congregants two antidotes to fear. These antidotes were faith and hope. Faith is the collection of convictions that one holds to and owns as their own even when those beliefs and convictions are under tremendous assault from the reality of a particular crisis. During the perilous and uncertain days immediately following the September 11th tragedy, many held to the fact that God was present, that He loved all people with a deep a lasting love, and that He would somehow give enough strength to make it through each day.

Faith

The faith that served as an antidote, dispensed from pulpits across the United States following the September 11, 2001, terrorist strikes, had various components. In my first book, a theological biography, I examined the key ingredients of a faith that carries one through tragedy and hardship. Clifford Hutchinson was a well-known evangelist in the tri-state area of Kentucky, Ohio and Indiana. This evangelist was carried through some very difficult personal medical crises because of what he believed about God. Hutchinson's life story is a study in persevering through difficulties. As a young teenager, a bone infection nearly cost him his life and limb. He was diagnosed with cancer in his abdomen when he was eighteen years of age and was given only six months to live. He was miraculously healed. He was involved in a deadly train accident while on his way to a revival meeting. The doctors told his wife that he would not live through the night. The last eight years of his life he was forced to take dialysis treatments to sustain life. Yet, despite the many storms Cliff weathered, he was very productive in his efforts to introduce people to Christ. At times, he seemed to be propelled over and through crises because of his faith. Consider the following ingredients of that faith:

"Cliff believed that God loved all people, and that this same God was in control of his future. The title of his preaching album, 'They Said I Must Die But God Had Other Plans,' demonstrates Cliff's conviction that God had already, a number of times, acted on his behalf to save him from death....In a sermon Cliff preached at the Evendale First Church of God, Cliff said, 'No matter what happens, I grab Romans 8:28 and hold on.' What Cliff affirmed is that the power to persevere comes in trusting that we have a good God who will make things turn out all right in the end, even when the circumstances make it seem that a positive outcome is impossible. Cliff believed that God's hand was at work in his life. His medical crises were not tragic events beyond God's all seeing eye or apart from his divine plan." [132]

In addition to the persevering faith in a God of control, the kind that serves as an antidote to fear, the faith of Evangelist Clifford Hutchinson was one that held to the conviction that God was a God of second chances. I wrote:

"Cliff believed that God was a God of second chances. He believed that God had given him—a gambling, dancing drunk the chance to start over. The evangelist never seemed to get over this opportunity to begin again." [133]

In addition to the above listed components of Cliff's faith, the evangelist's faith also proclaimed a belief that God was the God of the impossible; that He could do what seemed beyond human hope. Also, Cliff's persevering faith was one that held firmly to the fact that no matter how bad the crisis became God was always present.

Faith not only was useful for the crises of September 11th, but this type of faith also steadies us as we press forward through the fog of fear originating from the crucible of our own personal tragedies. The confidence that faith inspires, particularly a faith that contains the elements listed above, allows us to move through tragedy steadily forward, even though our future may seem dark and uncertain, even though we have no clue as to how God might turn these horrible events to our good. Faith is confidence in our Heavenly Father; it is a resolute assurance in the One who does our figuring out and worrying for us.

---

[132] Gary Agee. "A Giant in the Valley. (Clarksville, Tennessee: Reformation Publishers,1997),pp 81-82.
[133] Ibid.

124

Hope

In addition to faith as detailed above, Evangelist Clifford Hutchinson was able to press through the many tragic events of his storied life because of a strong hope that found its source in God. Hope is that set of divine wishes that faith reaches toward. Authentic hope is informed by God's will for the individual and for all people more generally. When tragedy visits, we are sustained because we envision a time when God will come onto the scene and will wipe all tears from the eyes of His children. Hope is supported by the word of God as well as by the conviction that God who loved the world wants to bring His children into the blessed life. In tragedy, all of these convictions may be drowned out in the dark waters of disappointment, discouragement and even despair. Hope says with the psalmist in chapter thirty, verse five, "Hold on. Weeping may last for the night, but a shout of joy comes in the morning." [134]

In Greg Smith's message of September 23rd from his pulpit in Birmingham, Alabama, he spoke the following words addressing the antidote to fear:

"The violence is not over my friends. And, as our response becomes more evident, this fact will become clear. Families are being separated. Even children in our own preschool are having fathers who have been called up… There will be times when confusion will occur. There will be times when our leaders, because they are human, are going to make mistakes. And we are aware that this conflict is not going to be brief. But through it all, God says to us today as He said to Joshua long ago, 'Be strong and courageous. Do not be terrified, do not be discouraged for the Lord your God is with you wherever you go.' Our God is an awesome God. He brings hope. We don't know what will happen tomorrow or the next day. But we do know who is with us. And I urge you to be strong and take heart, to place your

---

[134] I will leave it to the scholars to sort out the differences between faith and hope. Would it be fair to say that hope is what we wish for in the future, while faith is that virtue that moves us toward that set of desires?

confidence in Him, the God who will never leave us, the God who will never forsake us."[135]

Despair makes the individual in crisis lose the will to press forward. God offers hope for the person who is willing to reach up and take it. In that hope, we as Christians hold tenaciously to the conviction that right and good will win in the end even when there is not much evidence to support that belief.

Stephen Weldon touched on the theme of hope as he attempted to look past the terror of the days immediately following the September 11th attacks, to a time when the Lord would return and restore order to the fallen world, when heaven would become a visible reality.

"I can tell you more than ever that I am learning to anticipate and look forward to that period of human history when God will bring time to an end, and He will establish His perfect and eternal kingdom forever. I can tell you that I am learning to anticipate that time when I will be in that place where there is no sin that time when our adversary and his accomplices are thrown into that lake of fire forever and ever; that time when I will be in that place where there is no more suffering, death, mourning, crying or pain. Yes, more than ever I anticipate the reality of heaven, the reality of dwelling in that perfect presence and security and love of God with my Heavenly Daddy, and [I have] no apologies for such feelings. Friends, this is not pie in the sky... wishful thinking, and it is not the delusional thinking of some religious wacko...Scripture speaks of heaven as a very real place. Jesus spoke of heaven as that place that He was going to prepare for His followers. It was Jesus who said in John chapter fourteen, verses one through three, 'Do not let your hearts be troubled. Trust in God trust also in Me. In my Father's house are many rooms if it were not so I would have told you. I am going there to prepare a place for you, and if I go and prepare a place for you, I will come back and take you to be with Me that you also may be where I am.' Fellow believers, keep your eyes and your heart on the prize. This world is not all there is. We

---

[135] Greg Smith. Birmingham, Alabama. September 23, 2001.

have a hope; we have a future, even though at times things may be a pain now. Chin up, put a smile on your face, we win in the end. Heaven awaits those who trust in God through Jesus. We will have to endure a lot of garbage in the here and now, but please understand we have a glorious and perfect future awaiting us. This is why the Apostle Paul wrote in I Corinthians, chapter fifteen, and verse nineteen; 'If only for this life we have hope in Christ we are to be pitied more than all men.' True, for our hope is not just for now but also forevermore. And parents, will you please explain that to your children. Things are bad now; do not lie to them; but tell them that they can have a perfect hope forevermore. How about you?... Friends someday, and it could be soon, Jesus will come back and will judge the world. At that time, some will go into eternity without Him to a place where there will never be any hope. But those who have trusted in Him, they will go into eternity into the very presence of God. Jesus is going to come. It is going to happen. Are you ready? Do you have this hope? If not, place your faith in Jesus...Fellow believers, when we come to know this hope by God's grace and by engaging our faith, then it is indeed possible to really know peace in the storm, and the fellowship and presence of God in the middle of the battle; it is indeed possible to experience what David wrote so long ago in the Twenty Third psalm. Consider this anew. Can you say this: 'The Lord is my shepherd; I shall not be in want; He makes me lie down in green pastures; He leads me beside quiet waters; He restores my soul; He guides me in paths of righteousness for His namesake, even though I walk through the valley of the shadow of death, I will fear no evil for You are with me. Your rod and Your staff they comfort me; You prepare a table before me in the presence of my enemies, You anoint my head with oil, my cup overflows, surely goodness and love will follow me all the days of my life, and I will dwell in the house of the Lord forever.' Praise God! As someone has said, 'I do not know what the future holds but I know who holds the future.'"

Paul Dreger from Goshen, Indiana, made the following comments about hope in his message delivered after the September 11th terrorist strikes:

"What I want to talk about now is what we have all come to find, hope. Our reactions have been many this week: fear, anger, hurt and frustration. We have felt many things this week. All of them, one at a time, are enough over time, to defeat the human spirit. All of them combined are a formidable foe to peace, and to hope, and one's courage to face the future. Do we allow fear to win? Do we allow hurt to win? Do we allow frustration to win? We need not. For, as we have already shared this morning in worship, we, of all the people's of the earth, have reason to hope."[136]

A Tragic Goodbye

It was the last meal Jesus would eat with His disciples before His crucifixion. Emotions were high. He had called this band of believers to follow Him in order to usher in the reign of God. To this group of friends, and coworkers, He delivered a very intimate monologue. He began this discourse in John 14:1 with the words, "Let not your heart be troubled." It was for Jesus, and the disciples, a very confusing, painful and discouraging time. Not many hours after these soothing words were spoken, the heart of Jesus was broken as He experienced the worst of the tragedies of His life: He was abandoned by His disciples and friends, wrongfully accused, rejected and ultimately condemned by His own countryman. Finally He was crucified.

Before entering the crucible of this tragedy, Jesus spoke to His disciples some parting words. Words He must have said as He bit his lip to hold back a whole flood tide of emotion.

"In my Father's house are many dwelling places; if it were not so, I would have told you; for I go to prepare a place for you..." [137]

In the above text, Jesus speaks to His disciples of a house with many dwelling places, the King James Version renders these dwelling places "mansions." Given the circumstances, however, it is hard to imagine, in all of this talk of mansions, that the disciples heard

---

[136] Paul Dreger. Goshen, Indiana. September 16, 2001.
[137] John 14:2.

128

anything other than the cutting words "I go." They were losing their Master, Teacher, Prophet and Friend.

Not only was this to be a time of goodbyes, but Jesus was going to leave the disciples to carry out the overwhelming task of winning the world. How would they manage without Him? For they believed that He was the Messiah, the Chosen One, sent by God to usher in the kingdom. Jesus was their leader. They leaned on Him. They brought the tough questions and cases to Him. It is not a stretch to say that in the mind of the disciples there must have been a large dose of anxiety and fear associated with these questions.

Brad Sutter, in his message on September 11th, chose his text from this same incident in the life of Jesus. He related the following truths to his congregation:

"Let me just preface by saying this, that two thousand years ago Jesus spoke these words, but He could have spoke them Tuesday afternoon; they would have been perfect for the situation. He spoke these words just prior to His arrest and subsequent crucifixion knowing full well what was going to happen to Him. As He stared what some would call disaster in the face, here is what the Lord Jesus said...to His disciples, 'These things I have spoken to you...Take Courage. I have overcome the world.' .... Jesus spent an intimate evening with His disciples on the night that He spoke those words. He knew, as I have already said, what was coming. He had told His disciples many times what was coming, though they did not understand or believe. And, in that evening, you can read the words that He shares with His disciples, at least some of them, in John chapter thirteen, fourteen, fifteen and sixteen. He shares the deepest things on His heart, knowing that, prior to His crucifixion, these words will be the very last things that He will share. Then He comes to the very end of that intimate evening with His disciples. In fact, the very last words that John records in His gospel, the book of John, that Jesus said to His disciples prior to His crucifixion are the words that I have read in John chapter sixteen verse thirty-three. The very last words, the summation of that intimate evening.... In those few words I want to show you that Jesus did at least three things. First of all, Jesus stated

His purpose... Jesus' purpose that He states in this verse is that the disciples would have peace. That is what He wanted for his disciples. Church, that is what He wants for you today; that what he wants for America today. Peace. Is that possible? You say, 'Pastor Sutter, is that really possible? In the wake of the horrific events we saw on Tuesday, is it really possible that we could have peace?' Well, Jesus did not say this in the midst of calm. Jesus said this staring turmoil in the face, staring the cross in the face...Tragedy and turmoil test peace. Is that true? Think about that statement. You know what you can do in life is that you can put on a façade, a thin layer of external calm... it really is only skin deep. When problems and trials and circumstances such as Tuesday morning take place what happens to that thin veneer if it is not true peace? Man, it is stripped off and melted away. That is not the kind of peace that Jesus is talking about. Jesus is saying that in the midst of life's most difficult circumstances, you ladies and gentleman... you and me this morning, those people that are the victims of the tragedy of Tuesday morning can have peace...Jesus identifies a problem in this verse as well. Look at the middle of the verse. Once He has stated His purpose, that it is peace He says, 'In the world you have tribulation.' If you are reading the NIV, I believe it says that 'In this world you will have trouble.' Jesus is a realist. Jesus never tried to paint a picture that this world was going to be all roses and pleasure. Jesus recognized what this world consisted of... He said, 'In the world you are going to have trouble, you are going to have tribulation.' He told His disciples that would be so. He is realizing today; He wants to tell us that He is aware that we have trouble...He wants you to have peace. How is that possible? Here is a question,... 'Where do we look for peace?'... Do you look for peace...through affluence and wealth, financial security and prosperity? ... Can you build your peace on affluence, wealth and prosperity? Do you look for your peace in the military power of this country? Does it cause you to lay your head upon your pillow and rest in uninterrupted sleep knowing that our Commander and Chief at any moment could push a button and virtually incinerate any planet on the globe that is a threat to our country? ... Can you build your peace through health and long life, is that where your peace lies? Do you think about the unfolding of your life? [You take for granted] going from youth into young adulthood, and from young adulthood to young love, and from young love into young marriage, and from young marriage into career advancement, and from career advancement into young parenthood, and then from parenthood becoming a grandparent, then from becoming a grandparent into retirement and the easy life, just the normal progression of life. Is that where you peace lies, believing that you will have that normal unfolding of life and health? I am sure, and this is not meant ladies and gentlemen at all to be morbid; everyone of those individuals that went into the Twin Towers of the World Trade Center, Tuesday morning were confident in that they believed this day would end as the past days had ended.... Those that entered into the section of the Pentagon that lies in ruins...those that [flew] on those four planes that went down, they were all in the midst of the scheduled unfolding of their lives... Are we hopeless? Is that the end of the story? Jesus said in verse thirty-three, 'In the world you will have tribulation.' But do we just shut the book there? Some of you are shaking your head, no. Hallelujah. We don't shut the book. Jesus has not finished His thought. In the very next statement, He makes a transition, and He says, 'But take courage! Take courage!' He left us with a problem, but He [offers] a solution...Tribulation is not the end of the story. It doesn't end with trouble. Take heart. Take courage. And what is His antidote to the problem? He gives it in five words. He says this, 'I have overcome the world.' .... Jesus has conquered the world, and He can give you peace. He can give you a peace that can withstand everything that the world can throw at you, even the collapse of the Twin Towers and the destruction of the Pentagon ...He is bigger than all of this; He wants you to have peace today if you don't have it...He is the answer to this tragedy. He will speak into this midst of this rubble and bring about good...He has overcome." [138]

A Season Of Fear And Hope

---

[138] Brad Sutter. Anchorage, Alaska. September 16, 2001.

If there was ever a season recorded in the Bible where Jesus may have been anxious, it can be found in the gospel of Mark. The main character in this horror picture is the Lord Jesus Himself. The text, in essence, describes the unraveling of an individual's life. It seems evident by the end of the story that all light and hope had been extinguished from the stage. The bad news comes blow after blow during this tragic period in the life of our Lord.

In Mark chapter fourteen, verse ten, Judas moved away from the Lord in order to betray his Master into the hands of the religious authorities. This is only the first in a series of betrayals that Jesus suffered at the hands of disciples, into whom He poured His life. In verse thirty-two of this same chapter, Jesus walked to His regular place of prayer and asked Peter, James and John, His inner circle of followers, to join Him in prayer. In verse thirty-three, we find Him deeply distressed. In verse thirty-five, He collapsed under the incredible burden of sorrow. He asked His closest partners and friends to stay near Him and to pray with Him. In verse thirty-six, He prayed that He might avoid death. In verse thirty-seven, Jesus' aloneness is increasingly evident. His disciples slept as Jesus' world crashed in around Him. In verse forty-six, Jesus was arrested. In verse fifty-three, He was taken to be tried in the house of the high priest. In verse fifty-seven, some people lied about Him and gave false testimony to the religious court convened to try Him. The bad news was getting worse, and the darkness of tragedy was beginning to extinguish the hope in Jesus. The crowds began to spit, mock and physically abuse Jesus in verse sixty-five. In verse sixty-eight, the best friend of Jesus, His chief disciple denied Him. In verse seventy-one, He added to this betrayal curses. Jesus was truly and tragically alone. Not a single person in this text stood in His corner as a friend or advocate. The bad news kept coming.

In verse one of chapter fifteen, more trial proceedings. In verse eleven of this same chapter, the crowds chose clemency for a common criminal but, as recorded in verse thirteen, for Jesus they chose crucifixion. The mocking began in earnest in verse seventeen, with a crown of thorns thrown in for good measure. They bowed before Him as they laughed and sneered. All the evil ugliness that is reserved for the most despised and despicable was aimed toward Jesus. They beat Him with rods in the head, they spat on Him, and to add insult to injury they adorned Him with a purple robe. Not only did their physical abuse have a profoundly demoralizing effect on our Lord, but also the words of His own people cut Him like a knife. Sure, Jesus may have known that this awful day was coming, but He could not have imagined in His worst nightmares just how awful it would be. Jesus was exhausted, demoralized and doubting.

They crucified Him in verse twenty-five of chapter fifteen, a death too horrible to comprehend, even as the verbal abuse continued and intensified. At noon, in verse twenty-nine, Jesus was at death's door. It is curious that the Scripture makes it clear that darkness covered the land at noon. In other words, when the light from the sun should have been at its brightest, there was only darkness. This suffocating darkness extinguished in Jesus any hope that might have survived. Jesus died in that darkness, a darkness as black as any ever witnessed by any person throughout history. In His dying breath, in verse thirty-four, He cried out. "My God, my God, why have You forsaken me?" Jesus spoke for all people experiencing tragedy when he raised that question heavenward. Jesus, in this desperate moment, expressed a human grievance we all feel when we face personal tragedy. I am convinced that Jesus believed, at that critical moment, that God had abandoned Him. In that instance, in the mind of Jesus, it was over. He had been defeated.

The resurrection occurred in this atmosphere. When all hope was gone, the story threatened to end in tragedy and darkness. However, early in the morning, on the third day, a delegation of female disciples made their way to the tomb. Much to their astonishment, the stone was rolled away. God broke into the tragedy in a way that was wonderful, amazing and unprecedented.

The fact is, that every believer in Christ holds to the conviction that Jesus Christ, indeed, rose from the dead. We must confess this central tenet of the faith in order to become a believer in Christ. In confessing this truth, we often fail to realize its implications. God broke into the tragic event of the crucifixion and raised Jesus up from the dead. If

God was able to break into this hopeless tragedy, then each and every impossible situation in which we find ourselves must be viewed through the Easter event. Christians all have a resurrection bias. We see God was willing to be a part of the tragedy of Jesus' death, turning it to the good. We trust He will do the same for any person who will allow this resurrection power to be released in his or her life.

As we faced the tragedy of September 11th, it was important to realize that fear is never to be a debilitating force in the life of the believer. God wanted His people to live confidently and without fear of the future. This could be done according to the dispensers of God's Word by holding to faith and hope, antidotes of fear. In the final chapter of this book we will examine how ministers around the country encouraged their congregants to respond to the tragic events of September 11th. This study offers insight as to how we might respond to the personal tragedies that impact us all.

Chapter Six Questions For Discussion

1.)   Did the events of September 11th evoke a fear within you? Explain.

2.)   What do you believe is the most common fear for a child, a teenager, a parent, a middle-aged father, a grandmother? What responsibility does the church retain for addressing these fears?

3.)   What is your worst fear? How are you combating it?

4.)   Give Old Testament and New Testament examples of occasions when God addresses the fears of His people?

5.)   Do you agree with the author's notion that Jesus died without hope? Explain.

6.)   Describe a time in your own life when you seemed to be barraged with one bit of devastating news after the other. How did God help sustain you in that difficult period of your life?

7.)   When the author contends that we as Christians have a "resurrection bias", what do you think he means?

8.)   Despair, the author argues, immobilizes the individual. He or she is trapped in the tragedy and pain of a timeless present. What advice from the Scripture would you offer someone who has no will to move forward?

Chapter Seven
What Shall We Do?

"We do have a role in protecting the innocent, and in intervening in the world's behalf to protect the future. There is a serial killer loose in our world today, and I think we as a community, have a right and a responsibility to apprehend that serial killer, to identify who it is and bring him to justice. But let vengeance and retribution play no part in our noble ends... The presence and company of Christ will see us through, if we move about in the spirit of our Lord, if we find ourselves possessed by Him, if we are in His company, we will triumph."

Jim Lyon
North Anderson Church of God
Anderson, Indiana

"In the midst of the situation when our hearts are broken and we are overwhelmed; we are vulnerable to all emotion, we are vulnerable to solutions of the flesh, we are vulnerable to common sense religion, an eye for an eye. We are vulnerable to the cries of the crowds. We are vulnerable to look to the horses and chariots that we have designed."

Raymond Chin
Emerald Avenue Church of God
Chicago, Illinois

"Certainly right now one of the key questions in these United States of America is, 'What action should we take?' I want to tell you if this is a question in your mind, go to the Bible... When David in I Chronicles had the same experience that we are experiencing today, he went before the Lord....calling people together in order to pray and to ask God, 'What shall we do?' And David said, 'I will not go; I will not do anything until You tell me what to do'....We need to get before God and stay before God, and keep our leaders before God. Because many of them don't know how to go before God."

Manuel Holston
Martin Street Church of God

Lesson 31: Tragedy Is No Respecter Of Persons. It Visits The Rich And Poor, Pious And Sinner Alike

In the gospel of John, chapter nine, verses one through twelve, there is an account of an encounter between the disciples and a man who had been born blind. After this meeting, the disciples asked Jesus, 'Lord, who sinned, this man or his parents?' Jesus answered that no one was to blame for his condition. The truth that we may glean from this basic, but brief, bit of instruction is that tragedy visits the lives of the righteous and sinner alike. Tragedy is no respecter of persons. The fact of the matter is, that this world packs a large deadly arsenal of tragedies. They seem to be discharged into the lives of people without warning. Living a good and godly life does not exempt someone from experiencing trouble and tragedy in their life. The book of Job stands forever as a comfort to the godly person who faces one tragedy after the other feeling that God must be repaying them for some past sin. Job, in the Old Testament book bearing his name, suffered a number of heartbreaking tragedies, though he was the most righteous person of his generation. Job's trials and tragedies were not the result of God's judgment on his life. God's reasons for allowing suffering in the world are, even today, shrouded in mystery. When tragedy comes, it is hard to understand the reasons why God allows it. Suffice it to say, in the end, God in His own miraculous way, and in His own time, somehow brought Job to a wonderful end. God promised in His Word to do this for all believers.

Natural Tragedy

Some tragedies that visit nations, communities and the lives of individuals within these locales seem unavoidable. Some modern day diseases are genetic in makeup. The individual is born with the malady. No person's actions, or inaction, could have prevented the tragedy. In these instances, who can be blamed?

138

Natural disasters are another type of tragedy: typhoons, hurricanes, earthquakes, floods, tornadoes, mudslides, etc. One of the most awesome forces in all of nature is the typhoon. The amount of power released in one of these storms is incredible. The atmospheric and oceanic conditions that cause these violent storms are beyond human control. Yet, when these storms pound the coast of South Asia tens of thousands die as a result their surges, and the disease that follows in their wake. In these situations, there is no person that can be blamed.

Though disease and natural tragedies like the typhoon described above cause pain, it could be argued that they cause less pain than "choice-driven" tragedies. Those who are left to pick up the pieces after a loved one is maimed or killed as the result of the negligence or violence of a perpetrator, must not only deal with grief, but also an increased sense of anger and bitterness toward that individual or group responsible for causing the tragic situation.

When Someone Is To Blame

Yet, many of the tragedies that visit the lives of people are the result of a person or group of persons who choose to inflict harm, do violence and to terrorize others; these senseless tragedies are avoidable. That is part of the reason they hurt us so much. When the second airliner crashed into the World Trade Center, it became frightfully obvious that this tragedy was not merely an accident. Instead, it was the fruit of a well-designed plan to kill American citizens and terrorize the people of this nation by striking a blow at America's symbols of wealth and power. The realization that there was a band of terrorists, who were responsible for this violent act, immediately inspired a white-hot anger in people across this country. Pastors from New York to California, and from Alaska to Florida, united in one voice to condemn these vicious acts as scenes right out of a real-life horror picture played on televisions all across the country. Consider the comments of a few of the honest ministers in the movement not normally so moved, but who in the days following the strikes gave voice to this righteous anger.

David Shultz from Anderson, Indiana, shared the following:

"If you are like me, your emotions have just been up and down all over the place. I saw this remembrance in the first service and it moves me every time I see it. I am staggered by the photographs and images of the devastation and the loss... and then there rises up within me a feeling that [makes me] want to find whoever did this and just smash them to smithereens. I want to wipe them off the map. Do you feel that way, Angry?"[139]

Greg Smith, from Birmingham, Alabama, also expressed his anger and frustration at the people who committed this heinous act:

"And I've got to confess to you, and I'll just tell you my feelings on the whole thing. I suspect there is at least a few of you that share the same. My first reaction as we watched it on television was one of astonishment and dismay; this is a video game; this is a movie; this can't be happening. I have walked among those buildings... This can't be happening. How could this happen? How could these buildings be targeted; how could they experience such devastation? How could a one hundred and ten story building fall to the ground in eight seconds? Why didn't somebody see this happening? Where was our intelligence? Dear God, what about those people who were inside those buildings? What about those folks who were inside those planes? ... What was it like in those cabins during that time? What will happen next? Astonishment. Dismay. And then, at least for me, I felt inside of me an anger like I had never felt before. You can't do this; you can't get away with this. You don't slaughter innocent civilians, particularly women and children. And, I'll tell you preacher or no preacher, give me a cruise missile; give me a scud missile; give me a sling shot; I'll go over and take those guys out this afternoon."[140]

Lesson 32: The Way Of Anger Is Not The Christian's Path

---

[139] David Shultz. Anderson, Indiana. September 16, 2001.
[140] Greg Smith. Birmingham, Alabama. September 16, 2001.

Anger welled up in the hearts of many who watched the tragic events of September 11th as they occurred. It may also be said, that the closer we were emotionally to the victims of this tragedy, the angrier we became. Anger, when it demonstrates itself in this fashion, may just be the indicator of the degree of one's emotional involvement. Anger at the perpetrators of these violent acts against the United States of America was not an inappropriate emotion. It is permissible to be angry. I am quite certain that God was also furious over the cruel acts of violence directed against the citizens of this country on September 11, 2001.To be angry at perpetrators of this violence is not only permissible, but admirable. For in our anger, we must surely have been mirroring the same emotion that a loving and just God must have felt. Consider the directive given to the believer found in Ephesians 4: 26-27:

"Be angry, And yet do not sin; do not let the sun go down on your anger, and do not give the devil opportunity."

The writer of Ephesians gives the appropriate response. One who was angry at the perpetrators of this needless act of violence, was thinking as a Christian should think. Christians should become outraged when we witness violence and the needless slaughter of people Christ came to save. But when angry, know that the chance that you and I will make poor decisions because of our anger is great. We are to be angry, but we are not to respond to the perpetrators of violence in our anger.

In a number of cases across the movement, ministers pointed out that to respond in retaliation and anger following the attacks of September 11th would be wrong for the national government and wrong for the individual citizen as well. There was concern also that angry retaliatory strikes would be carried out against people of Middle Eastern descent.

In the following statement, Keith Gebhart speaks of directing one's anger toward the appropriate target, evil and hate, which cause individuals to act in violent and malicious ways:

"Once we start moving away from fear and toward faith, anger is something that rises up within us. The Bible says in Psalm 97:20, 'Be angry, with Satan, those who love the Lord. Be angry with evil, the evil one.' And that is whom we are mad at! …We are not mad at people who are of the Islamic faith. No more than they are mad at Christians because Timothy McVeigh claimed to be a Christian when he bombed Oklahoma City. We have got to direct our hearts where they need to be directed. To God for strength, towards evil, hate."[141]

Immediately following the strikes of September 11th, Osama bin Laden and his Al Qaida terrorist network was fingered as the group responsible. Because the members of this group were Muslim extremists, there was a real concern among the pastors surveyed that their people not retaliate against people of Middle Eastern descent.

Dave Shultz reminded his parishioners that responding with vengeance toward people who look Arabic would not be an appropriate Christian response:

"We are not after vengeance. We are after forgiveness. We must forgive. It is the lesson of the cross. So, whatever our country does we pray that they will somehow find a way to stop terrorism without killing innocent people. I don't possibly know how that can be done. And that isn't mine to decide. But, I know that as far as I am concerned, and as far as we are concerned, because I am your shepherd, we must let God's love flow from our hearts to everyone. We must not hold people who look Arabic at fault for something that happened by someone in a country that we assume was of Arabic descent. We must not discriminate. We must not jump to conclusions. We must be loving. We must be supportive. We must pray. And God will get us through this. Life goes on." [142]

How To Respond To Tragedy

Tragedy begs a response. People of faith are not exempt from all of the ravages of a world that is fallen. In many cases, the tragedies that

---

[141] Keith Gebhart. Hamilton, Ohio. September 16, 2001.
[142] David Shultz. Anderson, Indiana. September 16, 2001.

visit the lives of people could have been avoided had they consulted the Word of God and employed good decision-making skills.

As Gary Kendall from Olathe, Kansas, suggested in his message on September 16th we create most of our own problems and tragic situations. [143]For example, a young woman chooses to marry a man with a drinking problem. She wakes up one day and admits to herself that she is partly to blame for the dilemma in which she finds herself. A father finds himself in a custody battle with an ex-wife who seems to care more about controlling his destiny than the well being of this child. The truth is, to a great degree, poor decision-making led him to this point. Or, the middle-aged couple facing bankruptcy finds themselves in the crucible of tragedy, yet it could have been avoided if credit purchases would have been more carefully considered. Though, in many cases, tragedy can be dodged by making good well-advised decisions, in some instances tragedy is unavoidable. Sometimes, through no fault of our own, we suffer because of the decisions of another person or group of persons.

When the actions or decisions of another person causes us great grief and pain. What is the appropriate response? This question is a very difficult one. In Jesus' Sermon on the Mount, (Matthew 5:38-45a) the ethic of responding to violence and evil with kindness and love are established. Jesus said, "You have heard it was said, 'An eye for and eye and a tooth for a tooth.' But I say to you, 'do not resist him who is evil; but whoever slaps you on the right cheek, turn to him the other also. And if anyone wants to sue you, and take your shirt, let him have your coat also. And whoever shall force you to go one mile, go with him two. Give to him who asks of you, and do not turn away from him who wants to borrow from you.' You have heard that it was said, 'You shall love your neighbor, and hate your enemy.' But I say to you, love your enemies, and pray for those who persecute you in order that you may be sons of your Father who is in heaven."

---

[143] Gary Kendall, "What Matters Most." Olathe, Kansas. September 16, 2001.

Lesson 33: Violence And Evil Are Ultimately Defeated Only By Love

The text may be interpreted a number of different ways. The long and short of it seems to be that the cycle of evil can only be ultimately broken and conquered when confronted by love.

Dr. Timothy Clarke, from the First Church of God, Columbus, Ohio, seemed to pick up this theme when he reminded his congregation that "vengeance belongs to the Lord":

"Whenever something like Tuesday takes place, there is a natural tendency...for the beast in us to come out. Along with our shock at what happened, we are angry and we want justice. We want satisfaction. And let's be honest, we even want vengeance...And so....we see people throwing rocks through windows of mosques, and threatening the lives of anybody who looks like an Arab-American, all in a feverish, foolish attempt to get even. I want to remind this church and this country, this nation and this world, of what Jesus said. 'Vengeance is mine says the Lord, and I will repay.' I want to warn this nation. I warn this city; I want to warn this church that we are not to take into our hand what belongs in the hand of God. We will never do what needs to be done. It is not in our power to make some things right. But can I tell you a secret? If we learn how to turn it over to the Lord... He will work it out. I still believe that He is able to make your enemy your footstool. He is still able to bring down mountains; He is still able to raise up valleys; He is still able to prepare the way before you; And the God that we serve is such a great big God. He can even prepare a table in the presence of your enemy and your enemy cannot touch you, or hurt you, or harm you, or stop you; because when a man or woman's way pleases the Lord He makes even their enemies to be at peace with them. We need to remember, I feel like preaching, that vengeance belongs to the Lord. And we need to hear the Word of God... 'It is not by might, it is not by power, but My spirit.' The battle is not yours, it is the Lord's."[144]

---

[144] Dr. Timothy Clarke. "There is Still Hope." Columbus, Ohio. September 16, 2001.

Lesson 34: This Nation Has A Moral Obligation To Engage In "Just War"

The events of September 11th caused many in the nation to become actively engaged in the debate over how the nation as a whole should respond to the terrorist strikes. A fair number of ministers spoke about the need to respond to the attacks, taking some sort of military action. Even though surveyed pastors seemed concerned that the United States might be vengeful, or indiscriminate in its response, not one surveyed minister clearly objected to targeted military strikes against those thought to be responsible for September 11th. A difference was made in some cases between responding in hatred on the one hand, and responding in justice on the other. Church of God ministers across the country seemed in favor of a "just response" but not vengeance.

The Bible has something to say about the role of government in the arena of keeping the peace. The author of Romans addresses the need of believers to submit to the leaders of the state because they a have a God-ordained role, according to this passage, to keep the peace and to execute justice on behalf of the Lord. Consider the following biblical text:

"Let every person be in subjection to the governing authorities. For there is not authority except from God, and those which exist are established by God. Therefore he who resists authority has opposed the ordinance of God; and they who have opposed will receive condemnation upon themselves. For rulers are not a cause of fear for good behavior, but for evil. Do you want to have no fear of authority? Do what is good, and you will have praise from the same; for it is a minister of God to you for good. But if you do what is evil, be afraid; for it does not bear the sword for nothing; for it is a minister of God, an avenger who brings wrath upon the one who practices evil. Wherefore it is necessary to be in subjection, not only because of wrath, but also for conscience sake. For because of this you also pay taxes, for rulers are servants of God, devoting themselves to this very thing. Render to all what is due them: tax to whom tax is due; custom to whom custom; fear to whom fear; honor to whom honor."[145]

The following prayers lifted following the September 11th attacks seem to exhibit the conviction that this nation must execute justice, and that the President and leaders need wisdom in order that a path of justice might be discerned. Bill Ferguson prayed the following prayer from his Church in Washington D.C:

"Preserve the good judgment and discretion of those to whom we entrust the care of our nation and our civil life, remembering especially our President, our national and state leaders, our military personnel and public safety officials.... Direct us now and always, that no injustice arise in our search for justice."[146]

Mitchell Burch, from Vancouver, Washington, prayed the following prayer following the attacks of September 11th:

"Father, we are grieving for many things today. We grieve the fact that we have to live in a world that exists by power and by might and by military measures and needs. We grieve, Lord, that evil and sin, people who have ill will and deranged minds force nations like America... to maintain military... forces, to protect freedom. We're sorry about that, God. We know that this was not Your will or plan. But it is the will of man pushed upon man...I pray for this nation as we prepare to respond. We have all heard reports claiming that this attack will be a sustained attack. Father, I pray in this attack, that people all over the world, people in the areas where we will attack, would have the where with all and the ability to get out of harm's way. Lord, I pray that You, by divine wisdom, ...would help us find creative, strategic ways in which we could minimize the loss of the civilian life... It doesn't help our grief to see others suffer. Help us, oh God, to be accurate and be precise in what we do. Lord, I know it sounds so paradoxical, but Lord may we do what we must do without doing too much. Oh God, help our nation; help our world. Be with our military personnel.... Allow us to minimize our own losses and

---

[145] Romans 13:1-7.
[146] Bill Ferguson. "A Question of Value." Washington D.C. September 16, 2001.

casualties. We know, Lord that a great price will be paid, and we regret to have to pay it; so give us wisdom, discernment and courage. We thank You for Your presence and comfort in this hour, in the name of Jesus."[147]

Brad Sutter, of Anchorage, Alaska, prayed the following prayer demonstrating the desire on the part of pastors across this nation to see our government make the appropriate response to the terror strikes of September 11th:

"Lord, our President, George W. Bush, needs wisdom. Oh God, does he need wisdom! Lord, I have no idea, what he needs to do, but I know that You do. I know that You have the answers. Your Word tells us in Romans 13 that You have placed authorities in positions of authority for the purpose of justice. I don't begin to understand all the ramifications of that Lord. But according to Your will, we ask that You would give our President and the Senate and those that will be meeting to determine the course of action for our country... God, do not let them react and make mistakes, but help them to act in cadence with the leading of Your Holy Spirit as You grant wisdom and insight drawing out a path for them to follow. I pray that they would see it clearly and walk in it squarely."[148]

Earl Wheatley, Jr., of Meridian, Mississippi, offered these thoughts to his congregation on the Sunday after the strikes:

"As we go forward, we also must not go to hatred. Our goal as a nation is not to hate. It is to win this war. Hate hurts us more than it will ever hurt our enemies. When I pastored in Indiana... one of the lay leaders had been part of the occupation forces in Japan. As a matter of fact, he had actually been in the battle for Guadalcanal, and had seen the horrible things that happened there. After the end of the war, he went into Japan as part of the occupation troops. And he said, 'After being in battle against the Japanese, it was always so hard when they would stand before us and bow... I just wanted to knee them in

---

[147] Mitchell Burch. Special National Day of Prayer Service. Vancouver, Washington. September 14, 2001.
[148] Brad Sutter. Anchorage, Alaska. September 16, 2001.

the face.' But he said, 'I knew that I had to control that. Because the war was over, and I didn't want to let hatred be in my heart, even though my first instinct was for yet more vengeance.' He said, 'As they would bow I would force myself to be at attention. I would literally lock my knees as I saw them beginning to bow forward. I refused to let hatred have my heart.' To the best of my knowledge none of us have been personally impacted by the attacks on the Pentagon, or the Trade Towers. But, we need to pray for those who have been. We need to pray for those who have lost loved ones. We need to pray for those who are walking the streets right now, holding up pictures and posters… We need to pray that their wounds would not be turned to hatred. The calling that we now have as a nation …is to a just war. The Bible describes this. We can fight a just war, a war in which we recognize that there is some evil so great, some activity so vile, that societies cannot allow it to continue. We must stand up and defeat it. Hitler in World War II could not be allowed [to continue his reign of terror.] A permissive society becomes part of the problem. They literally add to the horror that has taken place. Strong societies must stand against evil at its worst and fight a just war. I want to remind all of us. We do not have to hate in order to win this war. We can be careful; we can be methodical. We can be constant. But, we do not have to hate. Don't let the devil get a foothold in your heart… And for those of you who have been wondering, Osama bin Laden is part of the Sunni sect of the Muslim faith. All Sunni Muslims are not extremists. They are not all our enemies. That is why President Bush has so wisely declared war on terrorists. This is not a religious pogrom. This is not a religious persecution. We have to remember once again that not all these branches are extremists; in fact we in America need to remember that before this day the worst act ever to take place on our soil was committed by Christians in the Oklahoma City bombing. Extremists who let hate in their hearts in the name of faith are dangerous. They must be stopped."[149]

---

[149] Earl Wheatley. Jr. Meridian, Mississippi. September 16, 2001.

148

Some in the movement found in related passages, such as Ecclesiastes 3:8-11, the justification for our nation to respond to these evil strikes with military force.

Tom Howland from Andover, Kansas, shared the following with his congregation after reading his text, Ecclesiastes 3: 8-11:

"I have purposely tailored some remarks to respond to our need of applying these truths to today and the days ahead. On your outline, please jot down 'Truth Number One. You gotta do what you gotta do....' Most Bible scholars believe that it was Solomon who wrote the book of Ecclesiastes, he was the wisest man ever to live, second of course, to Jesus. Solomon walked with God, and was an observer of human nature and he knew the things we have to do. Those things that he lists in those few verses are things that, some time or other in your life, you gotta do. Let's look at just two of them that speak to the questions we may have in mind as we look back on the happenings of last week. Truth one. This truth is stated plainly in the first part of verse three where it says, 'there is a time to kill and a time to heal.' At first, this statement seems to directly contradict what God has plainly stated in number six of the Ten Commandments; here Jesus said, 'thou shall not kill.' We find, however... no contradiction when we search out the meaning of the words... We discover that these Hebrew words used in these two applications are completely different. In the sixth commandment, the Hebrew word used clearly means that there is a prohibition against murdering another human being. To murder, means to kill someone in a premeditated way with malice for that person. The Hebrew word for kill in the Ecclesiastes verse, however, means to hit someone so that they may die. The element of premeditation and malice is missing.... We know it is never right to harm someone just for the sake of harming them. The word used in Ecclesiastes is also used in other parts of the Old Testament describing instances where people were killed when judgment was brought on them. In Exodus 13:15 it says that Pharaoh stubbornly refused to let them go, so the Lord killed every first born in Egypt. The other half of verse three it says, 'there is a time to heal.' This is a strong counter-point to the first half of that verse. Allow me to set up a scenario where this contrast

149

would be appropriate. We know that the attacks on the World Trade Center and on the Pentagon and elsewhere were premeditated murder. Against this type of attack, God is clear; it is wrong. It is a grievous sin against God. But suppose... that in the same smoldering remains of the collapsed building, a person who could be positively identified as one of the perpetrators of this crime was found badly injured, but alive. It might seem logical... to take that person's life on the spot. Right? Wrong. Even though we might think that we could...and do so justifiably; it would not be right.... I want to exit this point by asking you to pray earnestly for our country and our leaders, our President and all his advisors. We have heard so much talk in the recent days about immediate and stern retaliation for last Tuesday acts. Our concern should be that we not become like those people and nations that do such things. In fact, I fear that we are much like them already. Am I saying we should lie down and let the world walk on us? No. I am saying that we need to do things in an extremely deliberate... way. I personally believe that we need to seek help from other nations of the world. Proverbs 11:14 says, 'for lack of guidance a nation falls, but many advisors make victories sure.' We need to heed that. We can be sure knee-jerk actions will bring only more extensive and harmful reactions. ...You gotta do what you gotta do in order that justice be served."[150]

Lesson 35: We Must Avoid The Pitfall Of Bitterness

Bitterness

One of the necessities of properly handling tragedy, whether it be a national tragedy or one of a more personal nature, is not to let the tragic event we have experienced contaminate our spirit with bitterness. We must choose to continue to be gracious, loving people - even toward those who may have hurt us profoundly, perhaps even intentionally. All across the nation on the Sunday after the September 11th terrorist strikes, pastors warned their congregations about the

---

[150] Tom Howland. Andover, Kansas. September 16, 2001.

pitfall of bitterness and against retaliating against individuals of Middle Eastern descent.

Steve Chiles from Phoenix, Arizona, shared the following thoughts with his people in his September 16th service:

"We must guard our hearts against bitterness. In times like this, our hearts rally for justice, and we want a sense of making things right from all this wrong. In the midst of this tragedy, we must be careful so that we do not become like the very people we are angry at. That is why Paul says, 'Don't sin by letting anger gain control of you, don't let the sun go down while you are still angry, for anger gives a mighty foothold to the devil.'…We are just a bitterness away from those who performed this act of terrorism…I've got to help you understand, that this is not an act of Middle Eastern people; this is not an act of Arab people; this is not an act of people groups; this is an act of a few sick individuals. We have got to guard our hearts against being bitter and judgmental and lumping everyone who is from the Middle East into this category. We have got to be careful." [151]

Lesson 36: Forgiveness Is At The Heart Of The Christian Commitment

When we face tragedy like the attacks of September 11th, we quite naturally experience a wide range of emotions. One of the difficulties with which we had to contend during this delicate period of time, was how we were supposed to let go of anger. How were we to genuinely forgive? When tragedy comes as the result of another individual's action or inaction, it is imperative that we find the courage and love to forgive the perpetrator. The Lord's Prayer, meant to be a daily prayer, teaches us to forgive, so that we may in turn be forgiven. Forgiveness is the way by which we let go of bitterness. When we are unwilling to forgive, when we hold onto personal wrongs done against us, we simply cannot be made whole. By forgiving another individual, even

---

[151] Steve Chiles. Phoenix, Arizona. September 16, 2001.

prior to their asking, we are extending to that individual the same graciousness God over and over again extends to us.

The day following the strikes on the World Trade Center, I was visiting the hospital. During a break, I sat outside discussing the latest news on the September 11th strikes with one of my parishioners. He suggested that it might be a good time for the citizens of this nation to learn about forgiveness. I have to admit, I did not necessarily share his enthusiasm for this.

Having said this, I find it instructive that Carl Addison from Sikeston, Missouri, felt moved to share the story of Stephen with his congregation on the Sunday after the September 11th terrorist strikes. In this story, Stephen, a leader in the early church, was arrested for preaching and was subsequently stoned to death as a punishment. One would think that an individual undergoing such violent treatment would be angry and vengeful. The amazing thing is, that Stephen's response was to forgive this murderous mob.

Luke gives the account in Acts 7:54-60.

"Now, when they heard this, they were cut to the quick, and they began gnashing their teeth at him. But, being full of the Holy Spirit, he gazed intently into heaven and saw the glory of God, and Jesus standing at the right hand of God, and he said, 'Behold I see the heavens opened up and the Son of Man standing at the right hand of God.' But they cried out with loud voice, and covered their ears, and they rushed upon him with one impulse. And when they had driven him out of the city, they began stoning him and the witnesses laid aside their robes at the feet of a young man named Saul. And they went on stoning Stephen as he called upon the Lord and said, 'Lord Jesus, receive my spirit!' And, falling on his knees, he cried out with a loud voice, 'Lord, do not hold this sin against them!' And having said this, he fell asleep."

When a grievous and violent wrong is done to us, forgiveness allows us to move beyond the tragedy. That wrong perpetrated against us is no longer the lens through which we view our world. When we truly forgive, we give up our right to punish the one who has hurt us.

152

Following the strikes of September 11th, I also believed that justice needed to be achieved. After watching the news stories of Afghan refugees fleeing from the United States imminent attack on Afghanistan, however, I believed that the United States should attempt to feed and care for the refugees even as they attempted to rid the country of terrorists. In a letter to the editor I wrote:

"We were all deeply saddened by the brutal acts of the terrorists who struck a blow to our nation on Tuesday, September 11th. It is the moral obligation of our duly elected government to track these criminals and to bring them to justice…Wouldn't it be reasonable to take this same campaign one step further? How about feeding the Afghan refugees, even as we hunt down those suspected of the terrorist strikes on the United States? Could we not feed, clothe, house the refugees amassing on the border of Pakistan, even as we diligently search for those individuals responsible for the terrorist attacks on our nation? The overwhelming number of Afghan refugees fleeing major urban areas had nothing to do with attacks on the United States. Sadly, it is these marginalized people, orphans, widows and elderly men and women, who will suffer most from the events of September 11th, and whatever military course of action this nation chooses in the future.

Think about it. We, in this country, fear that we may suffer further terrorist attacks from a relatively small, clandestine organization…But think how frightened those citizens of Kabul must feel, knowing that the world's last remaining superpower 'stirred to anger' has their city in its missile sites. Make no mistake about it; the American people want justice. Justice, however, is far more than merely eliminating the terrorist threat to the proud American people. Justice also includes feeding and clothing those marginalized and displaced individuals living in Afghanistan…who are also, in a sense, victims of this attack.

The events of this past week have been difficult for the American people. Let us rise to the occasion. We are a great nation because we value every human life, American, Muslim, Jew, Christian, Hindu and

Buddhist. It behooves us in this crisis, to light the way for a world who is watching." [152]

Lesson 37: It Is Important To Get Right With God

The September 11th terrorist strikes took the citizens of this nation by surprise. People, who were uncertain about the future of this nation, flocked to churches in droves on the Sunday following the terrorist strikes. Because the Church of God Reformation Movement is evangelical in its heart, an overwhelming number of pastors took the opportunity to urge members of their respective congregations to get right with God, to be saved, and to become followers of Jesus.

Paul Mumaw from St. Joseph, Michigan, made the following invitation to his congregation:
"I think God was preparing our church for the events that have just taken place. Two weeks ago, Pastor Jim Gray delivered a sermon inviting people into a relationship with Jesus Christ. Last week... Pastor Moss delivered a sermon inviting people into relationship with the Lord, and at the conclusion of the message he invited people to make a decision... I believe God was preparing our church for what was taking place...Each and everyone of us has a seat in our life, it sits right in the center of everything we do. Just as pilots were forced from their seats this past week, we, in one way or another, have a pilot that reigns in our life; it is one of two people. It is either ourself, or it is Jesus Christ. If you have never accepted Jesus into your heart before, and acknowledged with your lips that He is God above, you cannot be saved. And the unfortunate tragedy on Tuesday is that many innocent people lost their lives, and met their Maker, and unfortunately they aren't living in heaven this morning. God gives us opportunities all through our lives... We never know when the day may come when our life may be taken. My question for you is, who is sitting at your pilot seat right now? Going to church for sixty straight years doesn't get you into heaven. It is inviting Jesus Christ into your heart. This is the only

---

[152] The Middletown Journal. 3, October 2001.

way we can come into a relationship with him. John 3:16 says, 'For God so loved the world that He gave His only Son, that whoever believes in Him will not perish but have everlasting life.' His arms are open and waiting for you. Are you willing to surrender your pilot's seat to allow God to come in and to be in control? Are you willing to turn the steering wheel over to Him? And if you are able to do so, and are willing to do so, you can live your life in hope from this day forward. If you are not willing to do so, I caution you that you do not know the day and the hour that your life will be taken."[153]

Mark Richardson, from Pittsburgh, Pennsylvania, expressed the following about seizing this pivotal moment in time in order to get right with the Lord:
"You know, one of the tragedies as I look at all of those lost lives is the fact that many of them probably went to the grave not knowing Jesus as Savior and Lord. In addition to that, many of them probably went to their grave having left a bad situation, maybe an argument on the way out of the house, maybe a bad relationship that had gone sour or was going sour. I am sure, as they were standing there looking at their own imminent demise, that if they could have gone back and fixed those things they would have. You see, they don't have the opportunity to fix what is wrong anymore. That is the saddest tragedy. They can't fix their soul condition; they can't fix their life conditions.... We have an opportunity to wake up, to realize that perhaps we are holding on to some things that aren't as important as we think they are. Maybe we have been hurt and we want our pound of flesh, but it is not that important. If the Lord were to return right now, if one of those planes, God forbid, landed in this church right now, would you be ready to meet Jesus face to face? That is keeping it real. At any moment you could meet the Savior, any moment. Some of us think that we have got years and years to get it together. The Scripture is so plain; it tells us that 'no man knows the day nor the hour.' You know that Jesus, when He was walking the earth, didn't know what

---

[153] Paul Mumaw. St. Joseph, Michigan. September 16, 2001.

day the Lord would bring the world to an end. He said, ' no one knows but the Father.' We don't know that we will make it home from church today. With that kind of understanding, can we afford the risk; of un-forgiveness, the risk of being out of the will of God, the risk of walking in sin and bondage to sin, the risk of not living holy before God, the risk of carrying a grudge, the risk of anything that would separate us from an eternity of fellowship with God? We walk around as if we don't think it could happen to us. But I want to keep it real. It can, and it does. The time to respond is right now. If you don't know Christ as your Savior and Lord, there is no better time than the present."[154]

Lesson 38: Because Tragedy Is A Part Of This World, Christians Must Share Their Faith

Terry Ball from Monroe, Ohio, highlights not only the importance of responding to God and being saved but he also celebrates the evangelistic fervor of one of the victims. In doing so, he reminds believers in the post September 11th world that we have a mandate to share our faith with a broken world that has lost its way:

"I was thankful to see Billy Graham in the National Cathedral… He said some telling things. One was that some folks who died in the World Trade Center went to heaven. He did not blanketly say all people have eternal life; all people are going to live in heaven. He didn't say that. Blocking our way to eternal life are cheribums with flaming swords preventing us from getting there on our own…No one goes back to Eden; no one goes and finds a fountain of youth. No one will find a cure for man so that he can live forever. God says nobody gets to know that way. That way is hidden…I watched a young man whose father was a flight attendant on one the planes that crashed…His father had been a policeman and decided that he hadn't seen enough of the world. He became a flight attendant so he could go all over the world…This young man talked about his father, and how

---

[154] Mark Richardson. "Keeping it Real." Pittsburgh, Pennsylvania. September 16, 2001.

he could not be sad because he believed in a God who gave meaning to everything. He was willing to say that, 'if this was my father's time, I believe He chose my father, because he said, he was a great Christian. I know if he was on that flight, he was on that flight to win a soul.'"[155]

Dr. Timothy Clarke shared the following remarks in his September 16, 2001 service:

"Now, if I am right, and the kingdom can't be shaken, then what does that say your response to that kingdom ought to be? Glad you ask, three things.

First of all, make sure you are a part of it. Because everybody talking about heaven ain't going there. Some folks are going to hell straight from the pew. It's going to get quiet now. See you think cause you show up...No baby. Coming to church don't make you a Christian no more than your hoopty sitting on the Lexus parking lot makes it a Lexus, no more than you sitting in McDonald's makes you a hamburger. You all are getting quiet on me. No more than you sitting in KFC makes you a chicken. Showing up at church just makes you an attendee at church. There are some of you all who need to make sure that you are in the kingdom. You are in a club. But the kingdom ain't a club. You came in here with your family, but you don't get this like you do insurance, on the family plan. You have got to meet Jesus for yourself. You need to make sure you are part of the kingdom. How do you know you are in the kingdom? You know that there was a moment in your life when you invited Jesus Christ to be your personal Lord and Savior. You confessed your sins, you repented of them and you turned your life over to Jesus. I don't want to hurt your feelings, but today is no day to play with you. If you haven't done that my friend, you are not in the kingdom.

Secondly, You ought to try to get as many folks as you can in the kingdom. I made a confession this morning because I believe in being honest.... You ought to be telling everybody you know who is not saved, there is a Christ who loves them, and wants to save them...If they die without Christ in their life, they are lost forever....You and I

---

[155] Terry Ball. "The Soul." Monroe, Ohio. September 16, 2001.

ought to do all we can. If Tuesday taught us anything, it is that you can be here today, gone today. And how many of those thousands of people went into a burning fiery inferno of eternity without God in their lives? And how many of them had Christian friends who never talked to them about Jesus? How many of those executives, corporate icons, had business associates who are Christians who gave them tax tips, investment tips, stock market tips and never asked them, are you saved? If the kingdom can't be shaken, you ought to be sure you are in it. And then, once you are sure that you are in it, you ought to try to get everybody you can to be a part of it. I want to deputize this church today to go out tomorrow, tonight at your restaurant, at your cleaners, at your supermarket, on your job, and share the love of Jesus with everybody you meet, because you never know when it is there last chance. Those folks who died on Tuesday, had you told them on Monday, 'You won't see Tuesday night,' would have laughed in your face. Today they are gone...

Thirdly, I must support it. Thank you for them eleven people who said, Amen. You all have been shouting all sermon long, and the minute I say support you all shut up. But that is normal, because you are afraid that I am talking about money and I am. Oh yeah, oh yeah. M.O.N.E.Y. mucho money. Yes, I mean money. Because if we are going to evangelize the world, if we are going to reach sinners, it takes money, to get on the radio, to get on the television, to build buildings, to hire staff. And if you love the kingdom and you want to see souls saved, then at some point your love ought to translate into you writing a check and giving some money for the advancement of the kingdom. Because, when you give to the kingdom you are giving to something that is eternal, that will give you results that are out of this world. There ought to be a total tithe of your life. Come on now. If the kingdom is real, there ought to be a total tithe of your life. You ought to tithe your time. You ought to tithe your talent. And, you ought to tithe your treasure. Everything you have ought to be at God's disposal. Everything you own ought to be available to him so that He can use it, and use to His glory." [156]

---

[156] Dr. Timothy Clarke. "A Word of Hope." Columbus, Ohio. September 16, 2001.

Some pastors went further with the idea of evangelism. For example, Keith Gebhart from Hamilton, Ohio, suggested that if the Church would have been passionately evangelizing the world, that America may not have had to suffer this tragedy. He shared the following:

"If we would have done our part over the last hundred years we would have won the Middle East to Jesus Christ. We would have won some of these hearts, Bin Laden and others to the Lord Jesus. But we didn't get them. But we want to get others."[157]

Stephen Weldon called the members of his church to respond to this tragedy by becoming light to the world during the very dark days following September 11th.

"The world is in desperate need of a breath of fresh air. The world is in desperate need for Christians to emanate and spread the beautiful and wonderful and hopeful aroma of Christ for those who believe…Many have said that we have entered into a new time, that we have entered into a new reality. In many ways, this is true but I propose that what has really happened is that the true reality of what has been surrounding us has simply been revealed. As painful and as unwanted as it may be, we have been given an honest glance into the spiritual reality of the world in which we live. Even though it was a painful and unwanted glimpse in many ways, it can be a very valuable tool in motivating us to tell a dying world of the good news of Jesus. Christians, with God's help and strength, let us open our eyes and see what God sees everyday, and let us be moved to be salt and light, and the fresh aroma of Christ that we have already been called to become."[158]

Maxwell Ware, of Columbia, Maryland, shared the following in his message entitled "It is Time to Seek the Lord: Multitudes in the Valley of Decision!"

---

[157] Keith Gebhart. Hamilton, Ohio. September 16, 2001.

[158] Stephen Weldon. Andover, Kansas. September 23, 2001.

"Joel described multitudes waiting in the 'valley of decision'...Billions of people have lived on earth, and every one of them - dead and living and yet to be born - will face judgment. Look around you. See your friends, those with whom you work and live. Have they received God's forgiveness? Have they been warned about sin's consequences? If we understand the severity of God's final judgment, we want to take God's offer of hope to those we know. The last word will be God's; His ultimate sovereignty will be revealed in the end. We cannot predict when that end will come, but we can have confidence in His control over the world's events....He sent us to be witnesses. He said you would receive power when the Holy Spirit comes upon you. He sent us to be witnesses in Jerusalem, Judea and Samaria, and unto the uttermost part of the earth. We are to tell our family, friends, co-workers, enemies the good news of Jesus Christ, and that it is time to seek the Lord."[159]

Dave Shultz used terminology from the Old Testament to urge his people to become "People of Refuge:"

"God wants us to respond by becoming people of refuge, people who have lived through tragedy and are able to be beacons of light and hope for others...God is our refuge and strength, but from God there flows this healing flow... we are the ones that are the conduits; what follows is that we become people of refuge, people of life. In the Old Testament there is a fascinating account of how God made sure that there was a place of healing and hope in that eye for an eye, and tooth for a tooth culture. If someone killed one of your relatives, you had the right to kill the person that killed your relative. But God established cities of refuge. You can read about it in Deuteronomy 19. There were to be three of these cities. And they were built on a different principle than the other cities. These cities operated by a different set of rules that God established for the purpose of compassion and justice. The rules were that not only would there be three of these, but they would have this special purpose...If someone killed another accidentally, if they went to a city of refuge the relatives pursuing them could not kill

---

[159] Maxwell Ware. Columbia, Maryland. September 16, 2001.

160

them until the facts were ascertained…These cities were built in such a place that they were available to everyone. They couldn't be so distant that someone running might not get to one. It says to make sure that the roads to the cities of refuge are in good repair. I love that. Is the road to your heart in good repair? Can the people of this world who are dying and now staggering under the onslaught of this tragedy, those who have no hope, can they find in your soul, in you, the drink of water that comes from Jesus Christ? Are you a person of refuge? Because the living hope of God flows out from us. We are God's ambassadors. We must be people of refuge. We follow Christ who lived by different principles than everyone else. He operated by a different set of rules that God established for the purpose of compassion and justice."[160]

The events of September 11th caused people all across the country to examine their relationships with God. Life again on that awful day in September seemed so fragile. A nation's citizens, many of them in church the Sunday following the attacks, were reminded of the fact that they would not live forever. One need not wait for a tragedy to right one's relationship with God. Do it while you may.

Chapter Seven Questions for Discussion

1.) Do you feel that the United States government responded within the parameters of God's will following the attacks on September 11th? Explain.

2.) Under what conditions would it be ethical for this country to use its military forces to combat evil in the world?

3.) How should the command given by our Lord to "Turn the other cheek" factor into our response to violence both individually and as a nation state?

---

[160] David Shultz. Anderson, Indiana. September 16, 2001.

4.) Do you know of an individual who was converted in the aftermath of the events of September 11th? Has that commitment proved to be genuine? Explain.

5.) List several biblical texts that speak of anger? What angers God? What constructive role might anger play in the life of the believer?

6.) The Bible tells us that we can be angry but that we should not sin? When does one move beyond anger to sin? Explain.

7.) How has this chapter shaped your views on how you might respond to personal tragedy?

Remembering: A Conclusion

Lesson 39: It Is A Virtue To Remember
Our Departed Loved Ones

As I mentioned earlier in this book, I considered writing a book at one time about lessons for living gained from insight gleaned from reflections in a nineteen-century cemetery. One of the planned chapters to that book I considered writing was titled "Remembering Those Who Have Past." It was during this same period of time that I became fascinated with the words and messages chiseled in the stone markers. These impressions left in markers were meant to be permanent. Shouted loud enough for succeeding generations to hear. These words were intended to defy time's tyranny. I imagined that these pioneers may have envisioned, as they stood at the grave of their loved ones, some person like me. In their minds, I would happen along and the stones would shout their sacred words to me. In this scenario, I was the intended audience. I would see the name of the departed, and as I whispered this name it would be carried on, an immortality of sorts.

By the time I had discovered this hallowed spot, however, what was intended to be an eternal shout, carved in stone, had become a faint whisper. For time, mildew and weathering had very nearly silenced these sacred words. What were these stones whispering? From these shallow stone impressions, I made out the names of the departed, and in one instance I could decipher a promise, one that since September 11th sounds very familiar. Here is an example:

Hattie Gifford
Jan 1, 1800
Died Aug. 2 1865
Farewell to thcc departed one
Our sorrows wake thee not
Sleep sweetly here the storm is past
Yet thou are not forgotten

There it was, a promise not to forget departed loved ones.

These words of love we have paraded out again in the wake of America's worst tragedy. Promises "never to forget" have made their way into books like this one, onto post cards featuring the twin towers ablaze, onto bumper stickers and bookmarks. We recognize that remembering is a virtue. "To remember is to make love," I once wrote in a poem. Yet, remembering is not something members of our present generation do very well. We have all but abandoned family cemeteries leaving off the age-old custom of decorating the gravesites of our departed ancestors. These forgotten family cemeteries, hosting relatives long past, "high branches on family trees," show the effects of our collective amnesia. The pace of our lives and the tyranny of the now have left no room for living, let alone remembering. There are barriers to remembering and honoring the departed even for those who are willing. We have failing memories, and often the effects of aging snatch away recollections from our past. Often, the devoted also have difficulty trying to pass their commitment to remember the departed on to succeeding generations. The above insights led me to write the following poem a few years ago about the death of my firstborn son, Jacob Ryan:

Only Heaven Remembers

A winter's walk rural and reflective
Crunching snow beneath feeling feet.
Here I am. There I was.
Shallow impressions tell the tale.
Ending up among cemetery stones breathing.
Calling names on high branches of family trees.
"Mary Randolf, Martha Taylor, Henry Gifford."
Stones, broken, misplaced, erased
Inscribed, a criminal condensation, "born-died."
Tearful pledges carved in markers…not to forget.
Shallow impressions then clear, now blurry with
The passing of generations and seasons –
Time's tour de force.

Icy blue I turn to return, falling snow
Covering shallow tracks.
I recall my eldest – the first to fly.
Life and love could not hold him here.
Tiny hands – a fourteen-day impression.
"Jacob Ryan Agee, Born: May 17, Died: June 1, 1991"
An expanding crater in my soul.

But winter swallows youthful summers.
Memories fall like flakes.
Time will snatch date, name, last his face
From my aging minds eye.
My children's children will lose me and mine
Illegible promises on misplaced markers.
My soul despairs, but hope answers,

"I am the God of Abraham, God of Isaac, and God of Jacob."
From the far edge of eternity I hear "Jake" whispered,
But only Heaven remembers.

Perhaps our pledges to remember the victims of September 11th will prove to be genuine. If they do, here are some suggestions as to how best to honor their memory:

1.)   Right our relationship to the Lord and to those in our relational network.

2.)   Recalibrate our priority structures.

3.)   Commit to finding God's will for your life and carrying it out.

4.)   Become a member of a Bible believing caring fellowship of faith.

5.)   Read and study the Bible and learn to pray and meditate on God's Word.

6.)   Seek justice at all costs.

7.)   Seek to selflessly care for those who have been charged to you as devotedly as the firefighters and rescue workers did on September 11th.

8.)   Commit to understanding and loving those of other cultures and faiths.

9.)   Follow Light and Truth.

10.)   Appreciate the people God has placed in your life to make it richer and more meaningful.

We remember the victims of America's worst day, September 11, 2001. But most profoundly, Heaven Remembers. For to remember is to make love.